AF434782

Under the Pomegranate Tree.

To my daughter-
i always want you to know
that you deserve all the love
this world has to give

To my mother-
the most incredible woman
giving, nurturing, and full of love

To my dear friends Kim & Tim-
i am forever grateful for all of the
wonderful memories that
i will forever cherish
and hold close to my heart

Under the Pomegranate Tree.

a series of poems.
Ariana Alexis Torrence

living amongst us all.

when they are young
you hold them and tell them
how monsters don't exist
but deep down you know
monsters are very real
they are all around
pretending to be your friends
pretending to be your lovers
pretending to be your family
coming in the forms of everything
you could have ever wanted
just to wait for you to fall for their trickery
so they can watch it all slip away
with grins so large about their wins
monsters aren't just in nightmares
they are apart of our reality
not all people love you
not all people care
some people are ruthless
they will pull rugs from under you
even when no one else is there
some will make plans to haunt you
preying on you
praying on you to fall
until the day you die

karma isn't real
trust me
nothing bad
ever
happened to the
bad ones
who wronged me
or maybe
the karma
was them losing me

wounded butterfly.

she then told me
how *i left her*
i abandoned her
like some kind of snake
from that day on
ever since that terrible day
but she didn't ask about me
w*hat happened after*
that day
what things even happened
what things i felt
what i had to go through
was hell and back
to get to my good place

my indignation.

when i was a kid
i buried my mom
i didn't bury my anger
my sadness
my resentment to others
or my grief alongside her

i buried the old me
the girl who held her tongue
the one that would not speak

the little girl who trembled with fear
when she was sad or angry
the girl who would rather sob than
say much of anything at all

now when i'm angry it sends
waves through the room
like an
earthquake

the temporary friend.

i lingered on the acceptance that
i'd never have
reaching for imaginary people
who would never hold my hand
i wondered about my mother
all the driving forces who made her
who she was
i wondered about whether people
actually loved me like they loved everyone else
or *was i just someone to pass time with*
someone who they could shell all their whole
life out to like they didn't have a choice
maybe no one was there for them
that's the turn in their stories
where i came along
when i was a child i barely had a favorite color
and even now when i say my favorite color
is red i wonder if it's all made up in my head
who am i and who will i be
will my acceptance come
or will i suddenly be somewhere sitting
alone drinking coffee while no one shows
their faces never around me anymore
when everyone's had enough of me
enough use of my kindness or my patience
just to use it and take it all for their vanity
act as if they created me like i'm some villian
in the pages of the lives of
everyone that i meet

then you said it directly to me
no one would ever want to see me
and
she would never
ever
ever
let me
live it down
it was enjoyment in her eyes
a sneaky smile behind the screen
she peered her eyes well on that day
i would never be the same
she found enjoyment in my suffering
a personal hell that brought with sickness
the ability for her to have wealth
like she could frame it and put it on a shelf
i realized the set up in her home
and the love that she claimed to have made
was all a fasad and is all now a lie
when you love a mother
you don't hate her daughter
they don't go hand in hand
if you don't hold my hand
you can't hold hers
mothers ride or die for their children
i know my mother always has
something for you to learn about
but there will be no next time
i forgive you because i forgive me
for not knowing just how i could even
cope with this grief

when the whole world cries.

i put my sunglasses on
just to keep my composure
just to avoid the exposure
i don't want to face the embarrassment
all the tears run down my face
and i'm feeling ashamed
i hate running away from these tears
i hate suppressing these fears
but what else can i do
sometimes people engrave things into you
just like glue
and when people ask if i'm feeling okay
i'd lie to you like i lied to them
i'm tired of people acting like they care
no one cared about the scars on her wrist
no one cared back then
why would they care now
don't feed me lies on spoons
and don't feed me empty promises
that you know you'll turn around and break
it's crystal clear to me that many of us
have to walk around with our sunglasses on
just trying to fake it until we make it
in a world full of a lack of compassion
a lack of grace
i wonder if people realize how bad it all tastes

a place under the tree.

faking emotions
pretending you've never been down
that road
seeing things
feeling things
i was never meant to feel
now i'm just supposed to let go
just let you go
right when i had you
in the palm of my hands
no i'm supposed to save you
i just can't let you go
then when our fingers slid
letting go
i suffer more than ever before
i'm supposed to let you drown
how
well now look at me
i'm supposed to let the gravestone stay still
and i'm supposed to move on
let it be
i can't let them get away with it
i can't let you be

the fruits buried.

some kind of competition
the years they had
she swore she could never win
all she could do
was
rip on her
to bring what they had
to an end
things unspeakable
she spoke them
more than you'd think
all while the fruit was
already dead
but she can never leave your head

the comparison feeds the ego.

no one's suffering is the same
many times- the birds flock together
to compare their pain
it's like some kind of game

10

stagnant dreamers.

we say morning instead of good morning
love you instead of i love you
bye instead of goodbye
in the moment everything seemed okay
behind closed doors were tears
the nuisances of all of our fears
living inside of us all for all of those years
i wondered why we didn't say good morning
why we said love you instead of i love you
as all our dreams went down sewer drains
as our everyday became a complaint
losing focus of everything
letting the bottle guide
falling on the guidance of people who despise us
falling mute on fake smiles and fake laughter
from everyone around us
just like them we feel the same
no connections just blame

the lessons of missing you.

grief made me crazy
and bizarre
and angry
because i know just how quickly
all the things you love
can be snatched away in one moment
you gave me your green eyes
you gave me hope for all of my dreams
you fed me love
more than anything
i'm grateful to have known
the strength in our love
life taught me a lot
love became everything
it taught me put my children first
it taught me love healed pain
amongst all suffering in this world
from one to another
i'd consider myself broken
if it weren't for you loving me
all the things that healed my wounds
where all the love bloomed
you're my bouquet
roses too
you're the sunshine
during storms too

you are the expert.

you have two choices
take control over your thoughts
or let them take control over you
be the artist of your life
or be the prisoner captive inside your mind
decorate your life or wait until
people come to decorate your grave
you can be the prisoner in their cell block
creating murals and finding dreams
or you can be the prisoner battling
the four corners of the wall
screaming helplessly with self-blame
self-ridiculing
self-loathing a life outside of those four walls
you can live in the moment
or let the next one destroy you
here goes many moments where we find
ourselves pointing fingers at others
drilling responsibility in the pain of our sore fists
finding hopelessness in the moments of our control
while the voids try and crack an itch
letting our dreams run sour without giving an inch
find the responsibility in the arms
our own where we hold ourselves accountable
where we find our truths in every battle
we ever struggled to compete
the only one in the competition is ourselves
finding the acceptance within ourselves
to find the ability to dream outside the origin
of where our dreams were all crushed

a lot of things remind me of you
my suffering for one
the things i'd imagined for myself
that i never received
in another universe
maybe
but even then addiction would still
drag you down into a pit of
helplessness
i forgive you
not for you
but for me
because *i'm supposed to be more*
than what you thought of me

in the meadows.

i envy how you can be a coward
and still call me a cow
i know all your secrets
the way you tell me i'm wonderful
just so a minute later
you can make me doubt everything about me
i see you lurking around
trying to snake your way back into my heart
like i might trust you if you were to cry
like a wounded child and that you are
if i knew how much it hurt you
like i might just accept you back
into my arms
you only accepted me when it benefitted you
but i'm supposed to act like i do no wrong
you'd show me off when i did well
leave me out when i did wrong
the punishment overall was the love
was not unconditional
the love was conditional
it came with terms and fine writing on the walls
if i ate too much and i looked fat
you'd tell me off
if i got into unhealthy relationships
you'd tell me i should've known better
when you never showed me healthy
after all–
how can i know better when you never
gave me better than what you had

maybe if i just stopped and figured it out
i wouldn't keep making the same mistakes
i wouldn't keep making myself suffer
the same fate
maybe if i cared more about myself
and loved myself
just as much as she loved me
i would be okay
i would love myself
but i'm not okay and i really don't know
sometimes how to be
i can't understand myself
i speak so much
i have so much to say
but i won't ever dare to tell people
about my pain about my suffering
i'll just sit there in silence
with a smile on my face

under all of my anger.

i wanted to scream at them
i wanted to yell at all of them
the one's who doubted you
the ones who fueled your suffering
the ones who dueled against your laughter
you were a mother with significant pain
i thought about what you would've wanted
since the very end
do i forgive them or do i leave
it makes no sense to carry so much weight
when they can't take back anything
i can't forgive you
i say to myself sometimes as i watch you carry on
but i must forgive myself
as a child all the things i didn't know
do i forgive you or do i walk away
i found it silly i had choice to make
anger has been the largest emotion
the biggest one that i could never fake

the sickness in time.

days
weeks
before i knew it had been a while
since you'd been near me
i missed the innocent you and
the boy who
found comfort in being with his family
i missed random
sporadic visits
where you popped up out of the blue
i never have visitors anyone
and no one comes to my door
i wonder what happens when time
plays a joke on me and 10 years
go by like minutes

the reality of my existence.

i was a protector since the day you passed
don't speak on the dead
don't speak on what you can't understand
like the others who when they ask
who have you lost
and they can't raise their hands
they just won't understand
and they can't even comprehend
we cannot be similar and our minds are unfamiliar
don't try to understand the holes
that fill spaces in my heart
don't try to understand the emptiness
i walk around carrying in my heart
you can't understand it
until it happens to you
you can't reach those shelves
where the weight of the pain
comes falling over you
like the lives that they had and the vessel
that life once would create is gone
when i open up my palm and i wonder
the creation of my life will someday be gone
what will i leave when i no longer stay
when my home is filled with all my stuff
when death comes knocking and says to me
that i've lived enough
i'm emotional because i have the gift
of feeling everything so heavy
it's sometimes too much
don't try and take away that place and make me
take up empty space where my heart needs to find
such grace

from this lifetime to the next.

grief is setting the table for two
it's holding photographs in your hand
crying late at night
it's remembering moments
and being stuck in
what could
or what used to be
grief
it both destroys us
and comforts us
it comes in the happiest joys
we share and the saddest
times when we wait for that
person to come knocking at our door
and when they never come
the abandonment fear
works it's way over to us again

cut off the control.

now here i go to the fire pit
throwing away the photographs of everything
the places where you made me deprive myself
of true happiness
the places where you made me compare myself
to all of the other children
when i never felt like i was enough for you
i must've been a burden to you
i'll sit here by this fire for some time
watching the fire burn as i get rid of every
single time i ever let you win
all the times i gave up and never fought
i would always let you win
you can't have my thoughts
you can't win this anymore
i won't let my memories fixate
on that negativity anymore
i'm done trying to carry around crates with
such heavy bricks
i take all the memories and i throw them away
here i am now by the ocean watching them
wash wash away

a dream of abandonment repetition.

each time i'd bargain about you in my head
thinking about how you never died in the end
i see you in my dreams
like instead of dying you moved on
you had a new family
you had a new home
i remember standing there feeling defeated
like wanting to ask you
mom how could you do this to us
i thought you loved us
now i stand here wondering
what would have been or could've been
would i have been happy losing you even
when you were still alive
watching you move on while you are still alive
or would fire burn inside me
like the fact that this all blindsided me
i'd be a fire pit of bickering and anger
of such a tragic non-demise
how i could visit you leaving flowers
at your doorstep or
i could leave flowers at your grave
either way this anger turns to rage
if i had to chose i don't know what i'd do
to leave you behind
on my knees i would cry
i can't do this without you but i had to
if i can't have your love who could
if you couldn't plant the seed of dreams
who would

a decade passed.

you
ask
me
what i'm so sad about
it was over ten years ago
what is there to cry about
you blink your eyes
and suddenly
time was stolen from you
a decade had passed
but not from my eyes
i was still like a child
crying looking out my window
i was wondering about the next day
when i thought we had so many next days
together
i was wondering about you
if you were going to get better
i'm still just as sad as i was
because the memories that we cannot have
life has gifted me so much love
but has deprived me of the love from you
i will always miss you

when you become a parent
to a daughter or to a son
you face this realization of the fact
you're bound to make mistakes
some that will make them happy
and others that may trouble them
like my parents before me
like the child who fell down and the wounds
went ignored
or the child who fell down and the father
yelled like the child shouldn't have been
so stupid to fall like that and hurt themselves
you wonder about what story they will tell
like my mother was a self-sacrificer
or my father was guarded
i knew i didn't want to be any of those things
i wanted to be a mother but for some time
i just didn't know how
i was frightened by the fact that maybe
i just wasn't good enough to be a mother
but if i was i wondered if i'd be a good one
my fears come from the roots of me
my garden would be filled with my tears
i want to be here for you
while i'm here for me
i want to heal together
so we can be as happy as we can be

liars eat lies for breakfast.

you can keep your secrets
keep your lies
but even the words you never speak
even the truth you push
to never think

we know

taking advantage of me.

i used to use things to forget
push it away
pushing all that pain as far as i could away
but then came the neglect
you putting your hand around my neck
the dragging me into another room
laying me down and showing me
that i can't forget no matter what
it was sickness and cruelty
what you did to me
i was just a kid
i didn't understand what any of that meant
i was grieving the loss of my mother
and you made it easier and easier
for me to never get it together
making it so i could never forget
when you were imprinted on my skin
i blamed myself so much that i would end up
hurting myself over and over again
i let people take advantage of me relentlessly
let them laugh as they rip holes through me
i let them do whatever they wanted while
i rotted consumed with guilt and fear
it's okay though
i finally made peace with these things
i know now that *i couldn't have known*

pray before you eat.

when i look at you the innocence has left
your eyes
for the young boy with the smile
is gone
your eyes are filled with a million
questions without a million
answers as to why
unknown why you live
unknown why you stay
i miss your innocence
and the bond we shared
now in your presence all i face
are arguments and regrets
i pray you find things you love
things that bring a smile to your face
when the world feels lonely
i hope you find something
something that can bring you grace

foundations of wounded children.

vulnerability has never been your thing
especially when your critic used to
tell you certain things
but you were taught to push away
the things that need to be spoken
taught to cry in dark places where the
sun would never shine
taught to push away
the things that needed and deserved to be spoken
it seemingly gets caught in your throat
it's a twisted knot
lump that you can't seem to remedy
but i understand you because i sat
at that table too and i saw it
unfold in front of your eyes
behind prickly cactuses
behind the mask
here lies the boys who were taught
instead of tears they were to just smile
being tough doesn't mean being strong
using drugs and alcohol to heal a wound
would only lead one to become consumed
the worst years of their lives
living in the shadows
while the other children who cry
get to live out dreams beyond the wounds
fathers wound their children
just by telling them to tough things out
it's like trying to breath through straws
later leading causes to the withdrawals

distance is 1.5 million miles away.

and i can't give myself false hope
thinking you'd come around that block
that you'd learn how to love me
in your dark spaces
when the silence became worse

when the distance grew further

and i outgrew you

i miss you
i was looking out my window
in my room
grieving
when it all was torn from me
hoping you wouldn't forget me
just us all growing up
we've been through enough
being without you both was tough
i was grieving every little piece
of what i had to become
it was like an eviction sign posted
at the home where i had love
a notice that someone was going to
knock on loves door one day
when i was away and then id never see
her face again other than at a wake
i miss you mom
i miss how you held me when i was sad
she made everything that was horrible
feel much better
the comfort in loving someone
just for it to be torn from me in my childhood
and when i cried i cried alone
all the other kids had their parents
all the other kids had their home
but then there was us

building a new detachment.

i felt torn away from you
i seen how the impossible
came to be true
when he told you
there was nothing he could do
it burned those bridges
when the way he behaved
was loose around the hinges
he was truly cruel
he wasn't fighting for me
he was done fighting for her
moved on within a week
like all of those years
were something he could never speak
i just don't think that's what love was
or what love could be
you showed me clear as day
years mean nothing to some people
who bury all of their pain inside
the hearts of others
your invisible suitcase still carries it all
even when it's been years and your children
still knew how much you ignored
your ignorance and the pain you clutch
in your fists all bottled up inside of you
i don't miss pretending wounds could
be healed with duck tape and bandaids

a plant watered with motor oil.

a lot happened
not a lot was said other than
hate that spit out of your mouth
you always shot me down
with your words
everything you said
every time you reloaded
and i'd stop in my tracks
and know
it's not a conversation to have
i felt frozen for years of time
trying to juggle between
reality and what could be
trying to understand why
i saw the potential
of everything to grown and learn
and why it only wilted
at my finger tips

i know now it's best to stay freed
so that people stop giving excuses to hurt me
so people stopped giving excuses to throw me
out in the streets
i didn't choose addiction
but it chose me
because in the dark of the night
when i was all alone
it lent me a hand
helped me escape my fates
it lent me broken promises
it led me to believe that it was the quickest
way to heal- was to suppress it
but now without it hovering over me
i can see how naive that was of me
trying to push the wounds out of my chest
is an impossible test
i can't get rid of what it did to me
i can't take away how it made me feel
it was much better to just accept it
for all of it's stupidity
rather than act rigidly
it was terrible and there would never be words
to piece together to define it all
but i accept it
and i accept me

all the love you give.

the unhealed version of me
wouldn't have chosen you every lifetime
much because everything you did- i'd question
my insecurities would eat me away
withering us away
i'd be like that 15-year old girl
right back to the time when i couldn't face
my own reflection
i now realize how much my looks had little to do
with you loving me for the deeper parts of me
like when you saw glimpses of my pain
and you would console me
holding me to my deepest core
still-i'd wonder if you'd lie cheat or hurt me
just to have me throw away these years
like empty promises that you gave me
but i wrap myself around again
to the realization that you love me
and you really really love me
the gift that life gave me after many years of pain
despite losing a mother
or not having a father
the gift was true love
and it both terrifies me and makes me whole
to love someone like you

caset tapes of my heart.

then they pressed play
without them around
without care
with ease
things looked simple
on the outside of the home
inside their minds
dwelling
dwelling deeply
on their own
i'm not tricked by this
fooled when others say you're innocent
they would say
you did the best that you could
but i just couldn't understand how
how me leaving meant nothing to you
how you never even changed my name
everything would always be the same
and that was the hierarchy of things
me at the bottom
the fact i couldn't measure up
that's why things could never be saved
i give up on us
gave up on the false beliefs
and the fact that my heart became misused
like you could pull my heart outside my chest
and you'd grab it sneakily just to abuse
when i rest my head on my pillow
my thoughts are
don't trust him he will only hurt you

the peace making trees.

there's something about
things we don't speak about
things we just hold
within us
inside us
holding our head high
under this great pomegranate tree
with all of this
gratitude
we avoid the hurt
to fulfill others
we stay silent in rooms
where we are
misunderstood
we laugh when we would
much rather cry
we isolate when we would
much rather tell them why
why it hurts us so much
this truth that we don't speak

dark room with my past.

i'm just someone
who can't even give you a straight answer
when you ask about my happiness
because certain parts of my life
bring me so much happiness
but a lot of parts make me quiet
and they put me in a long dark room
where i'm sitting in a lonely chair by myself
there's a voice asking me why i'm corrupted
why i make poor decisions
when i know my whole life is at stake
i really don't know why
but i know *how*
i'm just unhappy about parts of me
i'm deprived of a story where and if
and what i would've or could've been
i'm just so lost because *i should be so happy*
i should be thrilled that i have chances
but i'd take them all in my fist and clench them
until they turn to dust
so i can watch as the ashes fall to the floor
while i'm sitting in the lonely chair
wondering why it all fell apart
i rock this chair and rock with it for some time
sit down next to me so i can tell you the story
of how my past crept up near
brace yourself because some of the darkest parts
showcase the horror of such a filthy nightmare
you'd think it's an exaggeration
memories become such an aggregation
the numbness comes weighted

the world knows my truth.

the world
it reminds me much of a long path
never ending
no way to the comfort
of a nice home
it chews me up
and spits me out
it knows my pain and weaknesses
and plans to use them
against me
in my worst times
my worst days
it wakes me
from my best dreams
and my closest desires
it shakes me up
until it rattles my brain
just to let me know
i live and i breathe

i'll bring you flowers.

no one was my savior
it was supposed to be you
you were the one who would've saved me
from years and years of misery and suffering
and like an open wound
you open me up again grief
then you close me like a book then you open me
again each time it's another second look
even writing poetry reminds me of you
the little stories i used to write illustrations too
when you died all my dreams died with you
when you died all my life turned black and white
nothing had color for as long as i could remember
no child should ever lose a mother or a father
no child deserves to carry those things
when you left
i had to pack up my bags and leave too
i lost my mom
i lost my home
i grieved the loss of everything
and felt that i needed to stay clear from connecting
to anything that might give me a speck of love
i will be mourning your loss until the end of time
grieving the life that was stripped away from me
grieving the dreams that were supposed to be
labeling the gravestones by my ages
and dreams that never had a chance to be

clean up your act.

no matter how many times
i drive down that road
i make the same turn
each
and every time
i comptemplate the very balance
between right and wrong and i chose
wrong each and every time
perhaps i enjoy living
on the edge of sanity
i enjoy suffering and
ruining myself
i'm conflicted between finding true
meaning and fabricating my life on a lie
i clearly know how things end
i've envisioned them right in front
of my eyes

i couldn't help but think of you
rather than push you right
out of my mind
it wasn't even possible
i had to heal
i have to
i can't just act like it doesn't matter
you were just something small
you were much more than that to me
even if you wouldn't acknowledge
the same of me
it didn't hurt the first time
you abandoned me
the second time
is where i would fall
apart of me filled with all the grief
and the regrets i had
thinking of you
when you said that you loved me
but you never came to my door
at all

when you try to push it under
so snug
so hidden beneath
pretending nothing bothered you
pretending it meant nothing
in the end
but there's something
so meaningful
in the way that it will come back
full speed ahead of you
making you see it
making you feel it

finding myself.

if you asked me to tell you what i'm afraid of
i'd tell you its myself
see i'm the one calling all the shots
i'm the one who caused myself suffering
i'm scared that when people really
get a good look at what's in the inside
that they will really see me
they will also see the trauma
and the yucky bad parts of me
the way that certain experiences
tormented me for years until i was driven mad
i'm supposed to be something better than that
but sometimes you just can't
i've healed a lot of people
but i could never heal myself
i've given people the heart out of my chest
meanwhile i left myself out
all the winters when it was cold
that's how i would describe this
trauma can make you and trauma can break you
a lot of things can wound your heart
life will keep reminding you over and over
that you can't suppress these things
so each person you meet if they dig deeply
will begin to unfold the true meaning

making the connections.

when i was sad i'd wipe away my tears
trying to cope with grief years
with alcohol or letting voids consuming all my fears
anyway that i could fill a void
it would be filled to the brim of a cup
wipe my tears on the torn dreams
bricks laid on my chest
stack them up and
let my anger do the rest
let's take a walk so i can tell you about
all the things that made me *who i am today*
the trophies that i never put out for display
the ones i keep buried deep in my closet
all these skeletons that fill my closet
some would say *she struggled*
but they can't see all the things in my arms
that i juggle
i didn't ask to be this way
i didn't metaphorically want to have to choose
between the devil whispering things in my ears
or the angels witnessing all these tears

crime scene documentary.

silly of me to believe in you
when you stabbed me
in the back repeatedly
when you canceled me out
~~scribbled~~ my name out
you told everyone the
worst about me
made me out to be a monster
i'm always the criminal in your pages
and i'm the one
with the body bag
that
keep in mind–
you gave me
thanks for the framing
going to be a fun time explaining
explaining how
i'm not ACTUALLY crazy

the thickening plot.

i waited and waited
and waited
and waited
i waited for you for a year
every passing day
you never came to my door
you never even bothered to
understand me
all of our problems got ignored
each time i had an issue
you'd tell me go somewhere
go find a box of tissues
you couldn't care less about me
you abandoned me
and threw me out like i was disposable
over things you didn't understand
just to come back and reciprocate
to me what i just wrote and said–
i'm the narcissist in your book
the villian in your story
tell me again how i lied
about those who imprinted on my skin

never can ever happen.

i just wonder why you did that
and we never had a chance
i felt like my suffering started at the age of 14
really it started when you had me
feeling like a lost dog or the black sheep
that's what you did to me
that's all you made of me
seeing how i was irrelevant to you
what i thought of you meant nothing at all
why didn't he just want me
and why couldn't he just accept me
for who i am and who i wanted to be
i'd try so hard to pry at it with a crowbar
pick at it day by day
it never brought us closer
look at us to this day
i couldn't be what you wanted
i couldn't make you smile
still to this day now we are strangers
in this world and it makes me sad
part of me is glad because i know
it's all because what's inside of my veins
even then i don't know if i
would've had a chance

a villian's POV.

say something
around the lines of
that's just her
and i would agree with you
unknowingly
smile
laugh it off
silly
silly
me
unwillingly at times
rather than fighting you off
trying to get you off my back
keep thinking about what you want about me
like my life is some comedy
but the laugh i get is losing all those things
when i was only a kid
did you tell them those stories
how it all fell apart and you didn't
did you tell them how i felt
when you didn't feel it all like i did
or did you set up a stage
so you could walk up there
and cry those crocodile tears
like the rest of your family do every year
you can't trust a snake or a crocodile
i keep all of this information
in the back of head in a special file
that's why most of you are blocked
but i'll keep this memory unlocked

searching for answers.

i never knew my father
but i wondered about him
from time to time
when i was feeling misplaced and unloved
in a subjectively loving home
i found out the hard way
when i went searching for
answers about him
just to find out that he was dead
i had issues with trying to fix the one that i had
i was partly ashamed of the fact that
genetics meant so much
a product of my mother and my father
and all of it felt worlds apart
then when i found you
when that ended
i was in disbelief
but you were living without me for a decade
so i'm fine with the grief
i'll be there for you if you ever need me
if you ever need a shoulder just to cry on
if you need me know i'm here for you
even if we feel two worlds apart

when she judges
the dead
to make peace
with the living
she was so judgmental of you
just like you are of her
but don't think for a second
you both are worlds apart
your fears and anxieties
were hers too
she worried about him a lot
just like you worry about him too
just to lay up and night and wonder
about many things
whether you can save him
whether he would save you too
i think we both know how things end
and he knows it too
you can't put a bandaid over a bullet hole
you can't change your fate
you can't fix the way he copes
you won't get what you hope
i'm not mad at you
but i hope you know
what you signed up for
i would spell it out for you but *i just wont*

they heard you.

don't press your insecurities on me
thank you for the silence
filling my head with so much doubt
i laugh at myself
on the outside sometimes
punching the pillows of my beds
like i should've kept this all in my head
maybe i should've showered instead
rather than share this with you
all those times you didn't know what to do
was you telling me the story
that i needed to hear in the end

healing through trauma.

i'm still healing from many things
i'm working on myself
sometimes wondering how you are
but i have to stay focused
because *i can't fix what happened to us*
there is no time machine
i can't go back and i won't go back
i'm moving forward because that's all i can do
i'm not perfect
i have many insecurities
all of which you've used against me
i hated a lot of things about me
i was ashamed of the suffering inside
afraid to let anyone see what was inside
but i'm not anymore
i'm not a cat afraid of its shadow
i'm both deeply troubled by what
i cannot change
while also understanding that *i didn't know*
what i was doing
i couldn't know how to receive the love
that i longed for
all while i looked for love
in all of the wrong places

the trees that live forever.

you're the best part of me
you're so excited to see me on a daily
i come home to see you rushing
into my arms
you're asking for a hug and then another
you're goofy and loving and we have
everything that my mother once gave to me
when you were first born
the grief consumed me for some time
but now looking at you i understand why
when you love your child so much
you see all the beautiful things about love
you see how it can heal you and make you
whole on your insides
i was afraid so deeply because i saw a glimmer
of when my mother was here with me
and now looking into your eyes
i understand the love that she once gave to me
you're what makes me happy
you're my destiny
i won't be here forever and that's scary
because i just want to hold you forever and ever
i don't want time to steal me away from you
love can be so comforting but so troubling
because it's not fair
time just can't let that happen
so i'll love you forever in this world to the next

tears pour from my eyes
and i know–
when i'm silent
it's coming over me
the mourning
the morning you passed
became the death of me
i realized how lonely i truly became
every passing day
the world was spinning in circles around me
it wouldn't stop even when i asked it to
every day passing by
slipping right out of my fingertips
trying to force me to leave grief behind me
i realized from a young age
that nothing was going to stay with me
i was going to lose everything i ever loved
and that started when i lost you
i don't wish for children to know this
it steals away the fact that
you're young & you have time
but the truth is that we do not have time
we don't have much of it at all
so when fate decides what to do with all of us
we will lose it all
all over again along with ourselves

shaking the trees.

if all my fears were all in the same room
together
i wonder what they would say
probably something around the lines of
what happened to you
what did you do
then point fingers at me like i'm a criminal
they'd mock me and they'd watch me fall
they'd soak up my reactions
all while knowing about my roots
i came from damaged
broken
used
at least i've gotten used to them
if i just looked in the mirror
and faced my fears
maybe i'd see the truth
we are all prone to fears and anxieties
we are all prone to suffering
sick and twisted thoughts
that try and sneak around and steal joy
up from under our feet
in a dark room somewhere i'll just
accept the way my fears have withheld me from
true happiness and true love
i'll sit down in a chair and let them come here
let them show their face

a piece of me
will always be tied to you
hate you or love you
you'll always be in my dreams
so many unanswered things
i'm you and you're me
different life stories
different ideas
different dreams
what's known to me is our pain
our inability to
not change for each other
because
i'll suffer without you
or with you here

don't make me decide

never thought about all the things i'd miss
the way you smiled
the way you laughed
everything now every day now i will miss you
the way that when we both were sad
we had each other
we held each other tight
real friendships are hard
and life always seems to get hard
every passing moment you're not here
i think of how our souls were once so near
i'll be missing those moments
at my lowest you were there
it's not fair
when you lose someone you love
all you want is one last moment or one last call
but it wouldn't do you any good
not having your loved one here
you are the music in my ears
you are the laughter on the dark days
the sun when the darkness fades away
you are the sequins to my life
the sparkle that shines so bright
it's not fair that you're not here
my tears can't bring you back
the times of grief where i want to scream or yell
can't distract from the truth
that i can't have you back and that hurts too
there will never be another like you
a soul that lightens the room like you
pulling the rug of sadness from under me like you
you were a healer and i'm a healer too

there's little inklings
of her describing her flesh
as
gross
or
nasty
you harvested it
in the deepest parts of her mind
the depths of her believe
i destroyed the temple
i destroyed what was
supposed to be pure
cleansed
and
clean

she knew her place
she never asked why
silently she wrung her tears out
and hung them to dry
she hung her head lower than anyone
and no one seemed to care
she was projected as a problem
and then no one was there
erased from their life
she would never have an apology
or a reasoning or change
she would disturb the peace
she wanted them to know how she felt
but in the dead of winter
the ice will never melt
it would stay still for awhile
wait til she walked away first
don't count on people to change
don't count on people to apologize to you
we are all battling something
we are trying to get over someone who
burned us time and time again
but the seasons will come and go
and so will they

what i cannot change.

grief was a part of everything
the people she shared small moments with
the lovers that came and went
the fact that others could not love her
wherever she went
she missed the old her at times
the one who would let anyone in
now she's so guarded and so reserved
she practically never lets anyone in
she will sit alone if she has to
that's perfectly fine
grief did a number on me
it took away my happiness
if i was a puzzle many pieces
would be missing
even those who are dead to me
they took pieces from me
all while laughing in my face
people find it funny to come and go so easily
i felt this way everywhere i'd go
now i sit here in tranquility
where everything is calm
thinking of everything that once was
and not wishing for it ever again
i'm happy now with my family
i'm not thinking so much about you
but i won't pretend that it didn't hurt me

the real artist.

your art decorates all the places in my heart
your smile comforts my lonely heart
maybe love cannot be explained
because love is like outer space
you're like stars in the sky
the moon shining so bright
you are the dreams
the ones that you plant in everyone else's eyes
but you needed to know that you deserved that too
no moment makes it too late
nothing makes it too late to start over
looking at all the art that you used to create
you are a work of art
you are the sky and the dreams
i wish you believed in you
like you always believed in me
so you could be here to witness yourself believe it too
you take up so much space in my heart
the places where you were the first one
to make me think differently about my life
i want you to know that you deserved dreams too
you deserved to live freely and lovingly
you deserved warmth and comfort
not your minds tricks
not your negative thoughts that always convinced
i could never hate you
i could only ever love you
not the faults of our actions could tear that apart
not the words from our mouths could make me
feel that we should always be apart
you are always in my heart
a beautiful work of art

can i love who i am.

who am i if not the bad things i've done
who am i
if not the negative thoughts that run through
my head
who am i
if not for the bad things that happened to me
if not for the good that happened too
what is my soul consumed of
if acknowledging my sadness or greed
what is my soul consumed of
if seeing the pain i've given to others
in times where i felt conflicted by reasoning
what is my soul consumed of
the connections i've made
the way my soul is intertwined with yours
you and i
not everyone has that chance
to fully give themselves in
show someone the true raw stuff that most
can only scratch a little under the surface
i'm more me when i'm with you
then i am me when i'm alone
who am i
if not for the connections i have that will
forever last and send echos through
the earth when people forget my name
i'm more me than i was before
i'm more me than a child trying to do anything
anything to gain acceptance in any way
we both are the same

the darkness in our secrets.

i'm sure you've heard the expression
snitches get stitches
but what about the stitches that are infected
that never get removed after years of growth
and rottenness
eating me out from my insides
until i cry in a corner somewhere
my voice echoing for you
when you're no where near
you'd beat me and leave me in these streets
you'd beat me and leave me stitched up
so perfectly perfectly neat
asking me if i've had enough
the only stitches i ever got was from the wounds
and you making me your puppet to pull
i'm not a snitch for telling on you
after all the wounds you beat into me
i wanted something to beat into you
day by day giving me numbing agents
so that no one would notice the display
what will i do when doctors can't fix me
what will i do when people dismiss me
do i kiss these wounds
kill these wounds off with medications
and sedations
just to sedate this pain
while you're searching to arrange my framing
the wounds you wrote all over my heart
all over this skin
this time i cannot let you win

when we were at winans
due to the finance
i wondered where you were
something was going on
there was violence
stirred up with the silence
i was screaming inside
seeing all the pain
i was being guided
i was finding love
where things were divided

now here we are at the golden bridge
i'm walking across with you both hand in hand
we walk over to the fountain and i say to you
why would you just leave us like this
you look at me and cry you tell me how
someday i'll be seeing you again
when my own life comes to an end
you hold me in your arms
exchanging wishes in the fountain
i'm thinking to myself *how valuable love is*
how much i honor my daughter and my mother
so many years can go by time can escape me
but i can't escape time
when i open my eyes there's nothing more
that i can do than accept the realizations
they say *they take the good one's first*
that seems to be the truth
i'm tired of things being so unfair
if you could just be here
i'll remember to always hold my loved ones near
you never know when it's your last talk
or your last time going on a walk
i'll remember to honor the one's i love
because at some point i won't have a second chance
what will i leave behind when i'm gone
what people will think of me
and everything that i've done
will people cry as they look upon me
or will they smile knowing i lived a long life filled
with love and honor with a family
that i loved more than life itself

to become a dreamer.

i had decisions to make
my contemplation and my stagnation
could take over my life
or let my dreams guide me
live a life based on fear
like what people say about me is all i could hear
pressing my ears against doorknobs
letting people make me
and break me
and create me
or i could see myself behind the driver's wheel
driving myself to the finish line
the fine line between my fears and my dreams
the only one in my head is me
all the things that i have to say about me
those are the things that defeat me
with this preparation and this repetition
i am destined for greatness
destined to succeed
i can be anything if i make sure to prevent the fear
keep that fear outside my door
never let fear creep in
when the fear creeps in and the stagnation begins
i must be sure to not let this win
it starts with my dreams
and my ability to believe in me
more than others could ever believe in me
becoming a dreamer means defying those
who never believed in you

then the food gets cold
the coffee does too
i'm thinking of you like i probably always will
you're not here and i wish you were
i could find tiny cracks of things that i regret
like how for awhile we weren't friends
but in the end of it all
i never thought that would be the end
i wanted love and happiness for you
when you'd question how i felt
i'd tell you that *i loved you*
when you were down and depressed
i told you *i cared about you*
now everything feels fleeting
except the tears that run down my face
all the memories inside me
that take up so much space
i miss you and i miss our friendship
that now we are never able to have
memories we can't have
i used to love fall and so did you
don't do it because someone loves you
don't do it because i love you
i don't get how or why
denial worn on my face
a broken heart riddled
with all this broken space

let's grab coffee.

stay with me for awhile
so we can pass some time
talking about memories of those we hold dear
i'll never get to see them again
death is the reminder that nothing stays forever
death is the reminder to appreciate what you have
all this grief comes in waves
i would reminisce on everything i couldn't save
like how i'm holding you one moment
and the next you're turning to ashes
i'm sad and i'm hopeless sometimes
wondering how cruel and unkind
all the people i never got a chance to meet
all the people i never got to make memories with
and all the people who went to quickly
all the what ifs i had to leave behind
slipping right through my fingertips
when your mental health slips
wait wait let me pull you up
let me dust you off and make you brand new
whatever you need to do i'll do it
just to keep you here for another day
believe these words i say
come grab a coffee with me
before you think about doing anything
stay another day
stay another day

grasping the lost innocence.

children don't understand
when you tell them mom isn't coming home
they don't understand
when you tell them it's time to move away
just like it's hard to tell children
to put their toys away
children don't understand why they are chosen
last or left out
why when they need you the most
you leave them out
children don't understand the holes in the walls
or the walls you put up
when all you said was *it's okay*-but it's not
children don't understand or want to
when it comes to the pain and loss
we don't simply want it at all
children understand one thing
and that's the confusion where they are
left wondering if it was them all along
the blame replaces their confusion
the sadness replaced by their anger
children understand then and there
what it means to stop playing with toys
picking up vices to numb the crises
like the times they'd run to the bathroom
just to cry when they had no more shoulders
left to cry on
they grew up too fast and many of us know
this too well what it means to lose innocence
to lose such innocence and to lose your grasp
on the reality of death or what it might mean to die
what it meant to lose everything from your grasp

walking in those shoes.

i wanted to know what kept you up at night
tossing and turning in your bed
all the pent-up anger and frustration
knocking amongst the doors to your home
if i fit those shoes i could tell you what i'd do
starting from the root
starting from the core
working my way into stopping the damage
stopping this destruction from swallowing whole
if i was you i could tell you what i'd do
i'd start where it all began
work my way into therapy to stopping these
empty empty promises
empty empty apologies
i'm sorry
i'd stop saying *i'm sorry* and do something
do something
just do something rather than nothing
apologies don't heal anything
after you just got done shattering my plates
shattering the world around me
why does it take you this many years to figure it out
i turn around and look at you
seeing you still at the same place
all those times i gave you so much grace
well i'm done
you're doing nothing but hurting yourself
progress not perfection
but you do nothing to progress
you do nothing to progress
i'm done trying to handle all this stress

good things take time.

slow and steady
through the storm til i win
the comparison is a thief
like maybe i should be ahead
but i'm right here right now
where i need to be
this puts me ahead
my dedication and my sacrifice
all the weekends
kids partying while i try to get these
problems right out of my head
i'm a grieving child on the inside
i was looking out rainy windows
just a kid with dreams beyond the trees
just a kid who could barely read
i failed several times back to back
not learning from my problems
i failed all these fears back to back
contemplation
how i could do things quickly
but all these sacrifices
took many lives
stripping time away from these hands
right from the shine they said i had
i wasn't destined to turn these nuisances
into a royal hand

desperate measures.

nothing good will come out of
desperation
begging someone to love you
hoping they'd change
maybe they'd love you fully
maybe they'd change
crying
frantic
wondering
contemplating
what can i do
what can i try
how can i help them see to change
wasted so much time
wasted energy

different planets.

i left you in my

rear-view mirror

you

and all the others

right where you belong

i hate the way
i always give people
reassurance
when all they give me is pain
i gave my heart away
so many times
just to be running on empty
when i think about you
i hate you sometimes
i love you other times
i seen the good in you
way too many times
give me a moment
to recollect myself
you tore apart
my spirit
but you don't want to hear it

the race to get home.

paper thin boundaries
will have you running
for your life
just to turn around
and
welcome them
right back

the bee-keeper facts.

and *it definitely stung me*
like a bee
buzzing around me
when you went silent
it was clear who was the tyrant
you let me know my place
then your following actions
let me know it was a waste
queen bee
i forgave you
you never forgave me

burn it down.

two people living in a house
two people coming together
when things upset me
and you push them away
how can i be myself

two people living in a house
two people coming together
when things upset me
and you push them away
how can i be myself

the change of fate.

you made me love myself more
like i was actually worth something
i was a wishing well filled with beautiful things
i was the hope every morning at sunrise
in your eyes
that was enough for me to go on loving me
waking up trying to muster up my strength
to make it through these dreadful days
when i asked myself who i truly was
you knew me when i struggled to
you're the one who sees each one of my art pieces
smiles at me telling me *it's beautiful*
meanwhile i'm wanting to tear it up
destroy it
it wasn't enough for me
but it's more than enough for you
so i chose to be here each and every day
since the day i met you
you held my heart cautiously
made sure to run through jungles
with it wrapped up
so someone couldn't come up and steal it away
you made sure no one stole my joy or my smile
you'd hold me when my tears couldn't hold anymore
you'd hold me and watch me unfold
just so you could fold me back up
you make me see life as warm blankets
where like a heated blanket
i can choose to turn up the heat
when it's raining i can count on your umbrella
you'll be there to save me from acid rains
all these colds pains mean nothing now with you

memories escaping me like sand.

i forgot the warmth where you held me in your arms
i forgot the way your perfume smells
i forgot the way your laughter felt when it touched
the deepest parts of my soul
i forgot all the ways you made me feel okay
i forgot your voice
all the deepest parts of the connection we had
adulthood robs you more and more
day by day
night by night
i'm carrying around less memories
than the ones i used to have
no more childhood hugs from the one you loved
she's not here
deep down i wanna be a kid again
so i can feel it all the way i felt all over again
replay it just one day at a time
savor it like i do the pomegranate seeds
where you made me into me
photographs can't capture the feelings
the ones that linger underneath smiles and laughter
photographs can't bring you back to me
what i wouldn't give
what i wouldn't give
just to have that one last moment or one last chance
grief is sneaky
reminding me that things are here temporarily
but death-death is permanent
hold the one's you love close now because someday
well someday-you won't get another chance
you blink your eyes
you open your eyes one morning

many years go by
and i realize just how messy life can be
that year solidified a lot of things
that year told me a lot about me
i'm supposed to understand
my emotions
but they followed me around
like a scared ghost
until one day i confronted them
i can't get it out of my head
just how quickly
like a light switch
you turned it all off
while i was sitting there
drowning under the surface
gasping for air
right under your feet

he who wears a heroes cape.

now that he joined the team
he won't even speak about
what he did to me
some heroes wear capes
the evil i speak about
are the ones who never did

your like salt to my wounds
each time i think i'm closer and closer
there you go again-throwing salt to my wounds
you make me realize how all it takes is someone
bad for you to make you bad for you
i had to take a vacation from you
permanent vacations for these wounds
still there were reminders of you
everywhere i go there still is
like the fact that with my failure is a vision of you
like the fact that with my success
is my inner self-talk where you're telling me
i'm doomed
i can be enough for myself but never for you
still there are reminders and reminders
that i can't pass up because
they are road markers to my heart
every time i succeeded- i failed you
i'll fail you every time because my success
is something you cannot swallow
my success is something you cannot borrow
and make about you
oh-how difficult it must be
knowing i couldn't give it all away to you
just like you always wanted me to
in the matter of a few years i managed to both
sit at the bottom of the ocean floor
holding my breath
just to reach the surface and vow to never ever
let myself down in the end

when they ask who i am.

i won't even say their names
i won't speak it into existence again
was it when i was on the school bus
was it the parties or the alcohol
i can't tell the difference now
between scar after scar
i don't even tell the stories anymore
keeping them worlds apart from who i am now
i knew of a friend
i knew of a lover
inside it's who i once was
how much brokenness should i pretend i don't have
wondering if every passing person i meet
if they have the ability to actually read inside me
i pretend i'm not that broken
just so you don't have to pick up the pieces
i pretend i'm not that broken
just so i'll never be misspoken
because i'm used to being misunderstood
so when i say i'm not broken
i'm no longer broken
believe me- because that's the person i am now
feel free if you'd want to sit down and ask me how
i don't mind going into some details
small ones of course
about how i escaped the faces and the details
that could've done a great job
making me hate this body this face this place
everything who i am now
has nothing to do with who i once was
once upon a time lets skip to the time where i sat
for years just to uncrumple that paper

it was all one big lie.

i'm sensitive
they said
all the lies i was fed

i'm sensitive
they said
all the lies i was fed

she smiled brightly
blindingly
it was something out of the catalogue
of some happy happy
sappy magazine
no one could see through it
i could
it was some kind of sadness
some kind of twisted joke
happiness
wasn't really happiness
it wasn't even a thing

bleaked innocence.

i was only a kid
why did you make me see worth
based on this skin
i was only a kid trying to find love
just to be told you liked me
i was a kid there was nothing you should've liked
i was a kid my innocence was not to be tampered
leave it alone leave it be
no one knew at that time what this did to me
a lifestyle based on a soul
that would become deprived
the ruthlessness in your jokes about age
i wish my courage was as loud as it is now
from the times i couldn't muster up a whisper
i was someplace giving a taste
to the one's who never vowed to understand my soul
i was someplace where i did not belong
my innocence was to be contained someplace
in some container somewhere
where no one could get a taste
i grew up too quickly
a victim within the society and the environment
where inside me was this numbness
a falter inside my head
at that time i felt prized to be such a decision
a child suffering from acceptance i could not have
now as an adult i understand
keep the safety for the innocent
pry it with crowbars to make sure
things under the surface are not developing

they asked to see me
see what's under me
i was in the living room
just a kid
i was doomed
groomed
when he seen me at the town
i envisioned he drowned
he was caged for a few
but i'm almost sure
he's done this to a few

changing of the seasons.

my grief has not been easy
things have been hard
driving late nights in my car
i took myself back to the home where it all started
flashing all these memories back in my head
everything weighing so heavy on my heart
why did things end up this way
why couldn't you just stay
i know my siblings are thinking the same
things have never been the same and well-
sometimes i guess that is okay
grief changes you
makes you gather strength from within
i had to be the shine of my own life
focusing on all these dreams
just to build up a new life
one without you
now i'm not sure other people really understand
because they always tell me the same things
grief makes you isolated in your own suffering
no two people grieve the same

invading the safe place.

it was spoken
patience was weighing thin
they were coming over
just to touch my teenage skin

it was spoken
patience was weighing thin
they were coming over
just to touch my teenage skin

but we were best friends.

i miss the *good times*
sometimes
other times
i wonder
why you encouraged the wrong things
why you watched me drink myself
and make bad decisions
while you were
laughing in my face
the party was always fun
until it was over
it was always fun
until you didn't get what you needed
to survive which was
killing me off
some people don't want what is best for you
they come disguised as the seeds of evilness
that you keep around you

stay above the surface.

what's the story others tell about you
do people smile when they see you
do people cringe at the very sight of you
passing them by
i used to think having enemies was a bad thing
like- *how could i be so foolish at that time*
making mistakes to lose the people i did
but i learned that in the end of it all
i had lived and i had learned
be careful who you trust with your heart
be careful who you let inside your head
just as easily as someone can manipulate you
is as easily as they can tarnish you
is as easily as the story turns
you know- *the one they tell about you*
the twisting of truth is ruthless
but that's how it goes
but they cannot tarnish what is gold
do not allow others to keep your heart in the dark
do not allow others to luster
keep your shine throughout the time you have left
let others gather around campfires to tell stories
while you're out roasting marshmallows
minding your own

it comes in waves.

a home
filled with all my trauma
oh–
that's probably
more like
the ocean

the rotten part of my tree.

you are the
rotten voice
inside my head
you're old bread
the part of me
i want to keep
dead

take a number.

stop
telling
her
how
to
feel

if you wanted to be her
you should've gotten
in line like the rest of us

in these small towns.

you ever drive around someplace
looking out the window
knowing you'd be unwelcome there
you ever think about *what would happen*
if you dared to show you face in there

wrapped up in your branches.

the last night we spoke
you told me how you hope i find love
happiness
and the place where i belong
now the place i belong
is that inner child
where you held your children in your arms

what is love.

when i'm driving home
knowing people are still choosing me
i'm knowing that's a gift in itself
because people are so used to giving up
especially when things get hard
to not be burdened with the abandonment
that i was once living every day
faced with the scrutiny from those
who didn't care about my absence
and could easily forget my face

when fall comes.

when nothing worked
i buried it in the dirt
the words you said they really hurt
that night we spoke over the phone
and i told you *it's okay*
when how i really felt
was regret and doubt like nothing was okay
it was my knowing
i was dead to you
i was rotten fruit
i tried to talk to you but i was always on mute
i'm done trying
i left it all behind me
just for you to not show up
to a wake like you never had the heart
and you never made a single mistake
you never showed up for anyone
friends meant nothing to you
you meant nothing to you
now they carry around photographs of you
like you loved us both
but the both of us know that isn't true
you moved on without a clue
no second thoughts
no regret on the end of your sword
the one that was killing me off until the end
and they say some of the one's closest to you
will stab you in the back until their arms give out
people you love the most will give you up
and when they do they want you to keep
that lump in your throat where it all really hurt

the blended.

time goes by and the depression hits
as you become uninvited to family parties
looking at photographs on your phone wondering
how you couldn't be that important
recalling how others would tell you to just show up
but i don't want to be the unwanted visitor
i never wanted to feel unwanted
but i always seemed to be this way
time and time again
at a certain time i just stopped crying about it
i learned how to live with it and become numb
when a child learns their place
they will not forget
you can feel it in the air all around you
but inside you feel like you're suffocating
blood mattered more than anything
and i never knew that before
they'd brag about how good they were
how grateful i must have been to have been included
but i never was even back then
they'd smile at me but inside i was not deceived
i knew what i meant and that wasn't a thing
children know
children know
and time comes creeping forward
winters pass and summers come
realizations always sink in
i don't half love people because i don't know how
i wouldn't know how to treat children
with such a competition
one they could never win
i could never win after all

i want you to remember this
when you look at me again

i deserved better

i am better than that

how rotten of you.

how sweet of you
to let me know
my flavor in life
since the time i was trying
to figure that out

snakes in the garden.

you want to peel back my layers
like i'm an onion
then you want to ridicule my skin
touch the inner parts
you wanted me to know love
but you connected with me in the dark
you appreciated the fact of the matter
being the secret that it was
you appreciated what you did to me
to make me feel like it was my fault
grown enough to know better
than what you did to me
i didn't tell anyone at that time
to give you all that you wanted
i was drawn to the attention and the fact
someone wanted to please me with kindness
distracting away from the fact
you were like venom piercing into my skin
some kind of snake

there was that wall again
the one preventing me from connection
the one causing the affliction
when i'm looking at you and me
it took sometime to take that wall down
brick by brick
seeing professionals just to figure out how
how broken i was for all those years
now to my repair-
you can see me through this repaired lens

i'll never relax
as long as i'm holding my breath
a decade passed by
i didn't realize it
it was happening right
infront of my eyes
i was holding my breath
i wasn't letting go
i was holding it
clutching onto it
like it was my protection
i was holding onto it firmly
all of those weeds
the prickly ones
that make your hands bleed

then one day came
a special day
and i yelled–*let it go*
how freely i felt
i breathed
i awoke

it's like
not wanting to be in your skin
your flesh costs too much
the taxes to live there are
way too high
i can't afford to live there
in such
unlivable
unlovable
conditions

the peace maker.

i didn't come around here
trying to stir up anything
i came here with a shovel
just to dig up the truth
i come in peace
when offered apologies

forever friendly.

i miss your sadness
the way you spoke to me
i miss how alike we were inside
somehow
someway
we were the same way
i swear you were like
my soul sister
or something

quickly–
i realized how different we were
and then we fell through
just know by hurting you
i hurt a part of me too

and
deep
down

i'm
just
the
14
year
old
girl

missing her mom

the burning sense of blame.

sometimes you
just need to hear
it wasn't your fault
even if you believed it to be true
it wasn't your fault
well–
i could've

stop

it wasn't your fault

childhood friends.

now–
i wonder why
i decided to be friends with someone
who left me at my worst and came back
when i was at my best it was the way
you used it against me like some secret weapon
how different the summers
would have been
if we didn't betray each other

no photosynthesis.

maybe if you validated me
rather than shoving your
disappointment down my throat
until i choked
i wouldn't have needed to cope that way

and then there was that part
of the story
where she said and he said
i'm a *liar liar*
the exact words that you spoke
i wish you could read my mind like a book
just so you could have another look
the exact words that you spoke
i'm a liar liar
because
somehow
i asked to be groped
tell me again
how what happened to me
was all a joke

friend or foe.

i wonder why
you wanted the worst for me
and then you told me so
when they outed me
and you outed me too
pretending that you never
went through that same issue too

lets get to the root of it.

now
i'm sitting here wondering
what happened
to end up this way
was it the trauma
was it the drama
was it the dreams
washing down the drain
what was it
what could it be
whatever it was
i know you'll never see

survival instincts.

deep down
all she wants is to float above
the water
without needing a boat

deep down
all she wants is to float above
the water
without needing a boat

when the meds can't fix
what you lost
the pain you've endured
the hardships that
forever altered
your brain chemistry

everything became
stripped away
in the matter of
just
a
single
solidified
moment

the old me.

i couldn't understand
how i'm loved so much
so many people around me smile at me
people believe in me
more than i believe in myself
but still there was an itch
some form of emptiness in my heart
everything i went through
i must've died a few times
from a broken heart
each disappointment
each time i cried
still wasn't enough to put me under
i would call myself a walking corpse
everything was like a math problem
when everything keeps adding up
what they did and what i did
it haunts me night and day
takes me by the hand just to drag me
down into a dark pit
where i'd cry out to be saved
i'm still living through all the lives it took
for me to get things right

new beginnings in the garden.

i met with myself yesterday
i shook her hand
thanked her for being here
i asked all about the significant challenges
all the times she was stopped within her tracks
i listened and listened
as she told the story of all the ghosts
who came back to haunt her
she laughs and explains
how they saw success so this led them to taunt her
i'm impressed- i say to her
how'd you overcome
you're a survivor
how'd you build such resiliency
on top of rooted up trees
she looks at me telling me-
you just keep going
you don't give up hope

fat girl
i see you in the mirror
sometimes
laughing as insecurely
as loudly
as you used to

taking up so much

S P A C E

with your words just to feel
as thin as those
other
girls

you can take it all
lock it away
put it in a cage
but when you wake up
it's still there each and every day
people much older than me don't like apologies
people much older always look down on me
but in order for me to be who i am now
i had to learn about the hate you give
sit down across from someone in chairs
where i tear open this empty space
i used to keep for you
i would've reserved a seat for you here
i used to act like it doesn't hurt me but it does
when my self-talk became your self-talk
when i was only a kid
now i'm sitting here in this chair
running through all these memories
looking at the times when no one was there
i can see myself yelling
driving myself while i'm closing my eyes
i snap myself out of it and face my fears
because my life is like an hourglass
and i'm looking at you through the glass
watching myself every time
because you never gave me a chance
time is running dry now
it took me years to figure out how
to live without you now

losing you is worth it.

when you said you loved me
or you cared was it just because you felt
really
really
bad
for me
did you feel bad
when you threw me out
or was it just funny
to watch me
suffer alone
we never even had a conversation
you don't even know who i am
you clearly don't know what
grief does to a person
she's drunk fruit
she's off something
she's a terrible human being
i hear your voice and i realize
why you'll never understand me

root rot.

i wondered if that was the goal
was for you to hurt me
when i was hurting myself
was it your goal during the time
when we were friends
for you to damage me more
the persistence you must've grown
to make sure you'd hurt me
did it feel good when you said what you said
when you did what you did
it was shocking to me and i felt like you
would've cared a little more about my heart
i vowed to be more careful
sit in rooms that fill me with loneliness
than those people who judge me
there's nothing worse than being misunderstood
so let them not understand
some people are meant to love you
some people are meant to end up strangers
the people who listen are the ones who care
the ones who care are rare
as for those who don't care
when you make mistakes
they serve it on a dinner plate
all the shame they can tell you ate
it makes them happy and full on the inside
as they watch the people around them
suffering and unhappiness
become a pleasant surprise

keeping fall leaves alive.

please
please
understand
that without you
there can be no more memories
no more staying up late with you
no more laughing with you
no more comfort in your arms
don't let it win
don't let it keep you
don't let it show you glimpses
of made-up feelings
you hear me–
it's all pretend
you mean so much
that means so little
please
please
understand

when actions don't match words
and words are fed on silver spoons
nice vacations
cozy homes
and then tossed back and forth
like a football team
i hope you learn to
appreciate yourself
i hope you admire
the old version of you
the old family that was broken
for the parts of it that were
blooming
were
really
blooming

the trail left behind.

when you left
my world became silent
food lost it's taste
sleep became all i knew
an empty room with all your things
all this sadness turning into anger
replaying it all in my head
as the weeks go by from the times
people were asking how you are
people go silent
grief becomes more silent
we stop checking in on each other
making sure that things are okay
even when we know they can never be
people just wonder why you're always tired
the lack of motivation is an everyday occurance
dreams fade out in the background
as you're wandering around this earth
feeling confused and lost wondering how-
how do i live when the parts of me died with them
how do i live when i no longer know how
clearing out the home where we had a family
clearing out and boxing up all your things
picturing the last time you'll step foot in that house
wondering how everything came about
somehow i'm supposed to go on living
without you here

dust to dust.

just go ahead
go right ahead
and leave me in the dust

125

just go ahead
go right ahead
and leave me in the dust

like a movie
now i'm sitting here
reflecting on everything
that happened
trying to figure out
who the victim is
who the killer is
which one was me

honor the dead.

when you have to
please the living
more than the dead
because the dead provides
significant distress
to its enemies

letters to my enemies.

i remember getting off the school bus
kids were mean
especially when acceptance means everything
i thought home life was better
than school and the tears on my sweater
but i found most times i could never
find the same place inside me
when i cried i cried hard like my heart
was about to give out and break
from inside my chest
somehow it never did
i kept on living kept on moving on
from everything that you did
being back in this small town
driving around
driving around
seeing all the wounds that were created
from the very beginning to the very end
friends turned to enemies
enemies turned into my biggest fans
all my aspirations
and the weight all sitting in my hands
people still give me looks
i now know what it took
giving up on the acceptance
tossing it away like paper planes
tossing it away just to start another day
i don't care too much anymore
about what you think of me
stay my enemy stay my biggest fan
and know that it's okay to love yourself
more than you put energy into me

i just wanted you to know
so bad
how bad i felt
so maybe there would
be something
something
some speck
some little
small glimpse
of hope
that you'd come
around
and around
and around

i used to write poems
explaining how i was healed
or i was healing
but i realize i can't heal everything
i can't fix everything that turned broken
i can't explain why things happened
the way that they happened
why things led me to making those mistakes
i don't have explanations to everything
i can't explain everything
and sometimes it's okay to leave it there
and say that things happened
and that i forgive myself
i forgive me

all those years i learned
that love isn't grown in a garden
in the beautiful things we notice in life
love is grown in storms
hail storms
the unknown
the people who would go to hell and back for me
are the same ones who went through the storms
plenty of times with me
holding my hand guiding me
the mirrors didn't lie
the actions did deprive
each time
birthday cards that showcase the true love by word
and the word vomit that you'd wrote
only for me to find absurd
years i wasted by tv screens
hoping you'd just simply notice me
here i sit writing a goodbye letter
i now simply know better
as i go week by week trying to find all the secrets
to unlock my potential to ridding myself
of these internal conflicts that have the potential
to conflict me
it makes me sick but i try not to cry anymore
over people who never loved me not once
if you loved me living without me would be hell
if you loved me living without me would be hell
but it's heaven on earth for me
to not have to deal with me anymore

i was not at peace with myself before i met you
i didn't even love myself
but you brought both of those things out of me
helped me navigate my way back
from a deserted path
you helped me learn the good things about me
even when our relationship became flawed
we were a challenging pair
an unideal situationship
but i grew to understand you and love you
day by day we learned how to be kinder
to be wiser and learned why the earthquake
happened within ourselves
we learned unconditional love
we learned forgiveness and acceptance
i can't control you and you cannot control me
that's not what i want anymore
i learned it was best to let you either
destroy us or keep us together
now we are two peas in a pod
finding peace together
accepting that brokenness that we both
still have in our hearts
seeing it as a beautiful thing that life gave us
a chance to be who we are
together

devastation.

all the dreams i had
and yet
i still couldn't bring her back
it wasn't enough
all those tears
i cried

grief builds the love.

last night i had a dream about you
i couldn't make out all the details
like the look on your face
it was all a blur in my mind
that's what life does with my memory
snatching up the real parts of what i need
last night i had a dream about you
you come as my protector
my nurturer or my educator
you are the best part of my unconscious soul
you're the best parts of me that i know
my dreams give me the second chances
that life never gave
they give you the ability to live on inside me
freely floating around someplace
grief while so isolating brings families together
giving you the chance to share the joy
of love and life
when i wake up i think *put me back put me back*
all these dreams don't last
give me the chance
i just need one more talk with the one i love
all the time that passes but my heart won't forget
all this time that passes but my head won't forget
etchings made on my soul

then she gave me the truth
she said *i spent forever after that time*
guilt filling my head
eating cold dinner because of these lies i was fed
because she begged
when the men i talked to only lusted after me
and i would resort to squirming in my skin
i didn't love me and i simply couldn't
i looked in the mirror after that
i begged them not to leave me
just for everyone to hurt me in the end
you can't fix broken
and they knew what they were doing
they took pieces of my soul and crumbled
them up like paper and threw them away
my mind still plays tricks on me sometimes
like i had the ability to understand back then
when i was only a kid

axe throwing you and me.

you said we are family
you love me to the moon and back
but when i needed you
you didn't have my back
not at all
just like the rest
they said i should give it a rest
postpartum must have been some kind of test
your silence echoed through my head
letting me know we are through
i get it
i'll just get left
i was a mess

the haunting dreams.

that reoccurring dream
you never died
you moved on without me
you abandoned me

137

the way it goes.

i wondered what wound
would've hurt more
sometimes people believe that
life brings the ability to reconnect
with people that have hurt you
i find that troubling but true
but you'd have to forgive them
truly or you'd keep reconnecting
the past to what they gave you
everything i lost was worth it
other than the loss of you
i miss the things that brought me
suffering and happiness
a perfect combination of bitter and sweet

silence speaks to me.

the solitude of a room
filled with all the anxieties
running rampant in my mind
then suddenly
quieted down upon the
realizations
that
everything
out
of
my
control
is the reason
for my suffering

life passing you by.

the saddest song you've ever played
comes on
and then i'm thinking of you
i'm looking out the window
looking all around me
searching for you
asking for signs in the writings of my life
asking why you can't be here
living your life
death reminds us that everything
slips out of our fingertips
moments are fleeting away
when we don't listen to the people we love
we can't remember their favorite color
their favorite place
their favorite movies
or any of their favorite foods
once we are sitting there wondering
we realize the fleeting moments that escape us
it brings us so much value in the people we love
finding and discovering everything we can
everything about them
that makes them who they are
when you love someone and then you lose them
you carry that piece of them
forever in your heart

loudest in the room.

i found silent
dark
rooms
more peaceful
than loud bars
loud laughter
and the comments of those
around me
beating me to a pulp

all the bad things
i did could never
even come close
to the way
you make me feel
no one will ever understand
how it feels to be blamed
and ridiculed
for things that
burned me
time and time again

my shame
is still in there
hiding
spying on me
checking to see if i'm
staying in line this time
i used to be afraid to live my life
when i started making poor decisions
i thought the opposite like maybe i was
losing my life
but you can't change what you don't know
you can't know
well then–
you can't grow
i'm proof that you can be both a hot mess
and a hot commodity
i know a lot about suffering
i know a lot about healing
i'm still a work in progress
just like everyone around me

please
don't be codependent on me
i'm not your savior
your princess in shining armor
i'm someone else
someone just like you
someone broken
something that needs mending
then you blocked me out
played me until the end
exiled me out of the kingdom
but we weren't even playing pretend
i'm confused what happened
when you left without
saying anything
but it's okay
i'm not mad
you're a codependent queen

i missed you-knot.

i went down that block
so many times
sometimes i felt guilty
like everything
must've been my fault
i felt sad
questioning what things
could've been
then i think about how you cared
more about what everyone
thought of you
and that faded what you thought of me

even when i make
good decisions
a part of me grieves the
bad decisions i've made
i make excuses for them
like some kind of shield of protection
then i end up sitting there
soaking it up like a floor mat
realizing how messed up i was
how messed up i could've been
blaming people
for hurting me
like they would've known
should've known
how to love
someone
like
me

the shaming game
it's a real fun one in this life
to the next
who is better than who
who made less poorer decisions
who messed up the least
and survived the most
it's never about how they truly
felt inside
never about
wondering what
thoughts consume them the most
if it was-
i guess we would've come to understand
how equally ill we all are in some way
one
way
or
another

currently i just don't understand
what's wrong with me
years go by
i don't understand my voids
everyday my history haunts me
shadows hover over and around me
knowing all my secrets
hoping no one will ever find out
you burn into me
all my memories
flow through my veins
i'm a functioning depressed person
who curls towards rumination
about the bad things i did
my life feels like a chess board
and i don't understand how to play chess
every time i get coffee
i don't drink it fast enough
and it ends up cold as ice
life is like a rug waiting for my happiness
just so it can pull up from underneath me
i'm a functioning depressed person
other people come to me and say
they have no idea who they are
i laugh and tell them
i'm still trying to figure that out too

the outcasted sheep.

i bottle it all up
in my chest
everything you said to her
the names you called her
the terrible things you said
every time you wrote me off
i love being discriminated
against by the blood that's in my skin

then you said
she'd be ashamed of me
she'd be ashamed of what i did
knowing she's my mother
a bond like no other
playing on my grief
i'll let you keep that belief
you're not praying for me
you're preying on me
you're not good
from there i knew where we stood

new beginnings.

one day at a time
i miss being a child
when you were here with me
i'm tired of crying over you
while i watch everyone move on
without you
i can't move on without you
10-years went by but it feels like a dream
there are no time machines
there are no second-chances
there is no waking up in time
for me to save your life
and i've found that i can love you
and i've found a love as strong as
the one you used to give to me

he said
he's never loved anyone like me
when i was only 15
i was thinking it was all my fault
when he asked to see my skin
i remember i never told anyone what you did
i was just too ashamed of myself
to face the reality
i was looking for people to love me
in the wrong places
you filled spaces in me with delusions
that love was about terrible things
love was about me giving myself away
you invaded me
took advantage of me
now i truly understand why
i spoke to you

you taught me the world
but expected me to find love
and then expected me to
suppress addictions
ones that you said you never had
and expected me to understand
concepts i never would
understand
when you look into the mirror
both that darkness
and that lightness
reflect
don't deflect it
accept it

the neglected animal.

i'm a fool for love
i'll come crawling back
100 times and get beat down
100 more times
100 more times
like a sad animal
that wants love from their owner
i'll come crawling back to you
while you beat me down
then one day i'll run away
it'll hurt me bad
but i'll run really fast
you'll never see me again
and if you do–
i'll pretend you never
owned me in the first place

wrap me in your branches.

my safe place is a place where
you never died
you survived
you're here with me
holding me in your arms
i miss you
i sit there in our room that i made for us
wondering what you'd say
if you were here with me
what would you think about my daughter
that you never had the chance to meet
life has been kind and cruel to me
since you left us
i've been pretty cruel to me
i miss you so much
then i see your face and wonder
if you're checking on all of us
even when we think you're gone

the pitty party.

i pitty you
so hard
the way you're just
foolish
all wrapped up in this naive world
you think you could mold it
mold it all up like clay
well–
you're mistaken

fabricated love.

i just want to understand why
we all ask
as we sit there
being treated poorly
by those who say they love us most
i love you
they say
as they laugh when we cry
i hate you
they say as they watch our
whole world with them
crumble in front of their eyes
stupid me
we say as we weep
wondering *why*
you wonder why
i wonder *how*
how it came that i loved someone
who could never love me

the absence of you
follows me around
i think about it all the time
i wish i could take all of the good parts of you
bundle them all up
then gift them to myself
pushing them inward into myself
telling myself that's what i should be
but i'm more you than i am me
the bad and the good of you
it's like the world said
okay-she's suffered
but not nearly enough
the trails of my life show me
just how much suffering i'm designed for
both the good and bad inside
and then if i put them both on a scale
weighing them both
looking at them both in the eyes
i'd probably see the way
i've got a good heart
i've got good people around me
but life's just thrown me around in a circle
so i can replay out the bad memories
so i can conquer them or move on from them
like anyone would a bad dream

the comfort from my enemies.

a lot of things broke my heart
like the wrong people
whose shoulders i used to cry on
how could you
when i trusted you with my heart
how could you
when i told you things no one ever knew
why would you do that to me
snake your way in and out of my life
destructing me and making me lose trust in
everyone around me
many of the friends i had
didn't really find much meaning in me
in the simple moment of time
they'd throw me out or expose me
guarding themselves in a corner someplace
each time i hurt they would look for exit signs
it was simple to many of them
just to find a way out
being i knew what it meant to lose everything
important to me since so young of an age
that abandonment wound became huge to me
i cared about the people centered in my life
hold onto them and their kind hearts
i don't know what it was that brought others
so much enjoyment in my suffering
but i won the lottery but sticking to the ones
who really showed me love

and i'm supposed to pick up
my trauma myself
like shards of glass
broken all over the floor
then right after–
i'm supposed to glue them all
back together
piece them back together
over and over again
as i throw it back down
destroying it all
i'm supposed to forgive myself
with the blood all on my hands
i should be proud of who i am
as i torment myself
bully myself to unalive
like i hated myself for some reason
for living in this skin
but you can't take anything back
you can only move forward
and decide to go on living

avoidance to acceptance.

awhile back
i used to avoid the roads
where they lived
i'd take a different street
or simply stay on my own
it became comforting
for me to take
their road now
knowing what
i grew to understand
firstly
the tears that arose
it went through my mind
no one wanted me
they just threw me away
then came the reality that
not all people will understand the suffering they bring

the anxious being.

i'm tired of guessing
how anyone feels of me
what will become of me
will i even become something
or am i truly the monster in the mirror
that everyone always made of me
was i really the problem all along
time seems to stand still
the longer i waited around
for conversations we never had
moments we never shared
i realized my reality was
you were never
coming around
the abandonment became of me
like it always did time and time before
that's something you never had
visiting at your door

they tell you
live a little
i say live a lot
live more than a little
because a lot of anything
is of an abundance
an abundance of anything
is like a box of chocolates
a box of cupcakes
sweet things
life's supposed to be sweet
life's supposed to be happiness
even if you're not complete

i spoke lowly of you
like i didn't love you before
i said words out of my mouth
spoke them many times before
i'm stupid and cowardly
i could never say it to your face
the hurt and pain that you caused me
i felt like you deserved that fate
i was talking smack
but it was all a fact
you were never there for her
you were never there for me
not like how we needed you
anyways
you could possibly
maybe never
be there for anyone
or any of us anyways

welcome to my home.

let me show you inside my haunted house
let me show you a full tour
when you walk in this room this is the
shame room
there's photos of me from all the bad things
i did throughout my life that made me suffer
when you walk into this next room
this is the grief room
filled with all the warm fuzzy memories
of my mother and me
this room upstairs that's tucked away
is the part of me i keep intimate
only to myself
i don't want you to step in that room
it's my safety
but you can walk around everywhere else
that's fine
don't forget about the room of chaos
where all my emotions go haywire
the other room that's filled with my desires
the graveyard outside where i dug a hole
and put memories of things
i try not to mourn
i usually don't go to the graveyard
my grief lives inside this home

a full cycle.

there goes my life again
tangled all up in knots
strangling me one moment
releasing me the next
i'm not one for suicide
until it comes down to cutting myself down
from the rope that's holding my regrets
i'd probably die up there
strangling myself to death
while others scream
my one dream would be to finally be perfect
for everyone that i love
lose my old self and cut her free
watch her run away from the new me
but if you turn away as she runs
facing the inner fears inside of you
they end up coming true
you'll find out more about you

i was just a kid.

she probably did it
she probably ended it all
they say as
the grief stricken
children lay confused in their beds
crying in their beds
lying awake at night without
a clue as to how to live without them
they pull apart the lies
and eat them all up
piece by piece
they try to tell
me more about my life
they laugh
they smile
their mothers
lay peacefully in their beds
alive and well–
they are living
but speaking terribly
about the dead

postcards and apologies.

get over it
get over them
get over what they did
get over what they said
but i can't–
i can't escape the fact
i can't escape what it did to me
how it made me feel
how it tore me apart
the past is the past
the days are the same
time goes by
wounds all staying the same
i live without you here
it will never be the same
send me your condolences
tell me you understand my pain
tell me you're sorry

but

it will never be the same

boys must cry.

inside me *i was wondering about the boys*
oh-how boys don't get this privilege
this privilege of getting it out of their head
the distance was driving us away
like the distance between the scars in the sky
and the scars on my arms
fragile feelings unable to come to surface
adults telling children to wash wash it away
i was scrubbing my arms with my nails
while you were gulping it back over and over
fathers who tell their children *keep it all inside*
boys trying to understand themselves
while never knowing and embracing feelings
from the inside
i was wondering about the boys
so i sat in my room thinking about you both
all the time
hoping you didn't have to keep
sitting at dinner tables hiding your insides
but you told me that you're okay
i wanted to believe you while i was wondering
if that was the truth
your outside doesn't always show your truth
from vape pens to the suffocation
just a generation so lonely loneliness
creeping around in the nighttime
no rules and no made beds
breaking plates and putting them back away
saving these tears for another day
i was wondering about the boys
i'll probably always ask them *how they really feel*
because you never know if you have another day

a mockery of the leaves.

and yet they point fingers
at the people
who are wounded
while–
they themselves
are still bleeding

if you loved me
so much
why did you
do that to me
why do you have to make me
feel like that
why did you do that
why don't you just stop
hurting me

why don't you just

stop

hurting

me

the vulnerable one.

what drives me up a wall
are the walls you put up
to make sure not to
let me in
through the front door
i had to go around
to the back door
then i had to go in circles
when you weren't around
then i had to crawl back
and back as you watched
me become vulnerable
so you could never be vulnerable
not once
not twice
never at all

i woke from my bed with a knock on the door
he was speaking lowly about it
like she was someone really bad
i got up and went to school
thinking that nothing really happened
i put my head on the desk
i never slept
then they pulled me out of class
i thought it was a sickening joke
when they spoke of your death
i felt like they were kidding
it couldn't be real
i describe it still as my life changed
from then and there
somethings really change the course of your life
i was driving away in another family car
i was confused why my mom
couldn't pick me up anymore
why she wouldn't be here anymore
all the good ones go first
all the good ones
go
first

my addictions speak to me sometimes
like some kind of itch
trying to whisper to me to mess my life up
trying to whisper to me to do bad things
they speak to me when they know
i'm really down bad
deep down they know everything about me
they know my flaws
they know the voids that i fill
when i'm sad they offer to hold me
they offer to take my hand
just because they want me
suffering or dead
they whisper bad things
telling me to soak up my shame
soak it all up
turning me into mold
they tell me to live in fear
like i should tell everyone
tell the world that life has dealt me
a messed-up hand
they whisper me to me soothingly
comforting me until i face my regret
then they turn and laugh at me
laughing and pointing at me
like my life's a hoax or some kind of joke
i look stunned and shocked

rotten roots.

when i really got down
to the root of it
i realized most people
weren't really good at all
good for other people

sure

good for me

no

once you've grown
out of your roots
you'll find you've
outgrown
most of it all

a good way to know my place
by making sure
i'd feel out of place
it must've been a gift
a real jolly spirit uplift
you wanted to make sure it was known
make me feel unwanted
now it's reciprocated
i remember that day
even if i loved you
the bond was a waste
you can't give your all
to any of your kids
not the way you gave yourself
to all of the drugs
we could have a conversation
but it would probably be a waste
don't lie to me
don't lie to them
soon enough everyone finds out
exactly what you did
now i know my place
now i see the window clearly
nice houses and nice meals
don't always mean nice families

the pomegranate seeds.

pomegranates were our thing
the happiness they would bring
fall time
fall leaves
best time to get a pomegranate
from the heart of the trees
pulling the seeds out
wondering what it was all about
it's the best part
you always said
as long as you'd be around
i'd have someone to trust with my heart

a floral bouquet.

when i fell in love with you
there was no mistake
and we aren't ever
supposed to be perfect
you're not supposed to be
perfect for me
perfect doesn't exist
it's not possible for anyone or anything
i love you and you love me
that's enough

you gave me the biggest
gift i ever needed
i'll forever know
that i have found
my missing piece

empty meals.

was it charity work when you invited me
for warm meals
the disdain you must feel of me

this deep felt longing.

i just cry
for you
for the fact
you never had a chance
i needed you
so badly
but you couldn't see me falling
and falling
right alongside your path
if you just opened your eyes
opened them up wide
you'd see me struggling
hurting
crying

the statues molded from the inside.

the reason after all
was that i didn't want to
cause my own suffering
by being stuck in yours
when i seen you the last time
you screamed so much
you sat there speaking to the same one
who made you a product of who you are
a messy person
just like her
i remember telling her
i hope one night it's nice and cold
and she remembers her place
that rotten soul
i'll keep you right where you belong
you need to find better people
to place trust in
not from those that do nothing but hurt others
you need to learn that unconditional love
does not mean unconditional suffering
unconditional love does not mean
treat me *whatever way you*
want to treat me
that's not love

bowls full of insecurities.

the gift was passively
and actively
about my insecurities
it wasn't a kind gesture
i never said anything
i didn't want to pester
it upset me
it troubled me
that you didn't care
how you made me feel about me

play me for the fool.

when i said
i'll never speak to you again
it hurt-
but it felt empowering
because you hurt
everyone
everywhere you go
you destroy others
make them go limp
and expect them to grow
you manipulate
you tarnish
and you retaliate
you pretend and play victim
and it will never end

dead in the meadows.

when the good things
never happened
the good times
were never had
i lived with guilt
like it was at the root of my hand

and when nothing happened
in the dead of the night
she made herself a plan
to reorganize her life

just some food for thought
how were the years
were they kind to you
were they dry to you
like the sahara desert
did the nights turn into lines being drawn
where happiness could not be found
everything was in your ears
up your nose
i used to tell jokes but now i don't
you don't hear the echos of the pain
you're engraving in with daggers you made
words cutting pages of my childhood stories
garbage cans full of the dreams you found me
too full of
sneak your rugs
sneak your judgments of my passions
we went years without each other it was a drought
just to let you know what i'm really about
now you're knowing through your ears
but your eyes showcase your sourness
the sourness that i did taste
the words you chew up and spit out
end up on the plates of children
all this hate i cannot take
i don't like moving shaking homes
floor so heavy that it caves in
underneath this all i go in the gardens
malingering are the snakes
creeping up on me waiting to strike

treehouse decorations.

it used to scare me really bad
what you thought of me
i'd be laying on the floor
like some kind of rug
a welcome mat
hoping you'd notice me

starting the fire.

how much did it cost you
how much did it conflict you
how much did it hurt
when the cost of loss
hurts more
than the cost of
being tossed

my pomegranate girl.

it wasn't until then
that i was anyone's
favorite fruit
i was like the light of the day
i was like the hot sun shining down on her face
she loved me
held me down to the ground
she would move the earth
just so that she could love me
she's beautiful
incredible
you should see her soul
it holds me
when i'm low
helps me grow
then
lifts me up
like the wind

things without meaning.

i was surprised how quickly
five years ago
ten years ago still
became a struggle
there was something about how
i tried to bury my problems
and bury all my pain
that didn't sit right with me
my problems became my reality
they visited my door comfortably
dressed as nice things
providing me a sense of love
the voids became comforting
i wasn't complaining- i was hurting me
they appreciated how much i cared
about the things i wore
the way i looked
til the day i let those things die
i'm no celebrity and no one cares about
what things i wear
no ones asking for my autograph
no photographs
after the show was over
i'd sit there with these wounds
all skin deep
knowing about what i've done

lifetime of regret.

i'm angry at your wake
people keep coming in through the door
a revolving door
while my whole life
was practically thrown to the floor
people paying their respects
inside me my heart just feels dead
for years i replayed it all–all the details
where my life with you
would come to an end
and i'd go on living
even when–deep down
i felt this wasn't even real
most days i would find myself shrugging it off
it's no big deal
other like to tell you after a certain time
how it is you are supposed to feel
but living without you will never feel real or normal
i think the lesson is cherish everything
before our angels gain their wings
cherish everything
stop fighting over nonsense
before you feel the stings of their absence
leaving you with this defense
you cannot take back your words
be careful who you put on the end of your swords
you cannot take back your actions
behave with an abundance of compassion
you'll be left with a fraction of what you had
when every person around us
goes the same place in the end

the hallow tree.

i couldn't tell you
how many times i sat down in the shower and cried
every time i lost pieces and pieces of people
who completed me on the inside
the sun stopped shinning around here
and i stopped caring when
you stopped coming around here
rather than growing together
we only ever grew apart
both sides of our souls battling each other
packing bags and moving rooms apart
now when people tell me they will leave me
i try to not give them a single piece of my heart
keep it safe and tucked away
while the deeper parts of me scream and cry
taking me right back to the home
where it all started
and i'd tell you let's just live another day
because i don't want to be without you
unless i really really have to

i'm done begging
like a peasant
i'm done climbing trees
while you broke down my branches
i'm done asking you
to water me
to follow me around
complete me
if you don't want me
well–
that's quite okay
just know the disaster
you left
within me

give yourself a hand
a loving one
for enduring suffering
for enduring the pain
for seeing how it felt
and knowing how to grow
allow yourself to feel it
allow yourself to talk about it
and don't feel like you can't let it show
cry a little
cry a lot
feel anger
feel lost
feel confused
feel things a lot
let it go and grow
you'll be doing this
to heal from a lot

before you knew it
days
weeks
years
went by
no one talked about it anymore
it was old news
it was wiped clean
they seen it as a clean slate
clean from their vocabulary
cleared from their dictionary
nothing was destined of their fate
cleared from their bedtime
stories and workbooks
just like they'd want us to think

one baby girl
all the sunshine
she brings
could heal the entire world
from its bits and pieces
that's what she does to me
my sunshine girl
she's a dream

it's an honor
that those who know me-
appreciate me
those who know me
know who i want to be
they water my dreams
care for my flowers
wish the best of me
and cheer for my branches
they tend to me
shine light on my trees
allow the rain to come
whenever that might be
they don't push it away
shun it
or tell it to stop
they would tell you
let it be
it will rain tonight

the tree nut.

if you're going to be crazy
do it with class
tell them why you care
about something
be glad that they asked
and when they don't agree
allow them to say so
but stay crazy my friend
the normalness never lasts

reasons to be here.

you can be sad
but don't stay there
you can be mad
but don't stay there
don't become comfortable
or complacent in your own suffering
do not eat from bowls that will poison your mind
stripping you away from the inside
do not build a home
based on things or situations that made you feel
like a bag of bones
there is a brutal battle out here
a life where we take in all the air of our fears
waiting to strip you of dreams passions pursuits
just don't get comfortable putting on those
old beat-up boots
if i could tell you one thing it would be
the wounds on your skin signify the specialty
of your story
the scars on your arms tell the times you got lost
simply got lost trying to figure out exactly
who you are
do not stay there
stay here
make sure you stay a visitor there
you are one moment or one day away
from figuring out everything you needed
on the hard days know being here means
you have succeeded

self-love.

you see that home-i point
you see that home i built that
surely i didn't build homes
i wasn't an architect
but the place inside me is the home
the one i built from nothing
when everyone used to betray me
when everyone exiled me out
i got me
i give me a big hug thanking myself
i'm everything i needed
i'm the brand new floors
the brand new doors
i'm the safety and the place
where everything comes together
i cross my arms and hold myself
i'm the furnance in the winter
i'm the student and the mentor
if you get a chance to step foot in here
make sure you appreciate the comfort
of freshly baked cookies and warm hugs
give my heart a warm tug
a good home could always use good people
to take care of it but mine can still hold it's own
this is my safe place

there's nothing more to say
nothing more to do
i can't get over you
but i'll grieve you
i'm fine with loss
i'm comfortable
with the fact i gave you up
and won't let
what you said
about me be true

i'm healing
i'm changing
i'm accomplishing
i'm thriving
all with feeling
all the feels
doing all the doings
i'm humanizing
my experiences
all meanwhile
i'm becoming
becoming strong
powerful
resilient
empowering

you are not
their vision
their story of you
the picture they painted
in their head
or what they made of you
you're more than that
better than that
and something bigger
than they will never know

i'm grateful you're here.

you mean something
not just something–
a lot of things
you're filled with
dreams and passions
and so many stories to tell
make sure that you tell them
please
tell them a lot

the first selections.

standing near the headstone
watching as the wind blows
thinking of our favorite songs
i know you gave me your green eyes
i'm gifted with your insight
never did i think id be losing you so soon
it was way too soon
watching all the girls smile
laughter along side their mothers i stand in denial
as i sit here at this headstone wishing you were here
how come they get to keep theirs
never did i think amongst my worst fears
i'd be out here kissing headstones
wishing you were near
their sending their condolences
i'm wondering if it's consequences
for everything to be stripped away from me
did my luck just seem to catch up to me
there goes my pomegranate tree
there goes my honey bee
there goes my heart outside my chest
there goes my favorite parts you'd always see
all the girls holding their mothers
i think about and wonder
do they ever think what could happen
or what could be
as their dreams begin to ripen
death begins to point fingers at them
don't choose them
i don't want them to lose them too

the rage room.

a room of everything
that troubles me
and everything that makes
me go mad
a room of everything
where my anger
turns to sadness
and my sadness
turns into resentment
and pain

then i finally said
forget it
forget it all
forget what i said
forget what i saw
i don't need to say a word
i don't need to do a thing
just leave you in the dust
like we were never a thing
no history
no museum of confusion
no guessing the meaning
no art gallery of exclusion

the visitor wears red.

it should've disgusted me
what he said
but instead
i just felt curious
now that everything was gone
and everything was dead
i felt terrible for it
seeing it in my mind sometimes
what i did to her
was i supposed to know
how to protect me
now that i know what i know in the end

all the versions of me.

these tears are temporary
just like the night showers in the night sky
these failures are temporary
when tomorrow brings more opportunities
somethings may sit with me for awhile
but i can find comfort in sitting with them
invite them over by the fire
so we can each take turns telling stories
i always found laughter in my dark times
laughter in my darkest crimes
maybe because they made me become me
each day i'm a new person
i feel different that's how i know i'm certain
sometimes when the bad things
coming knocking at my door
i knowingly invite them in
other times i mock them and watch them cry
i watch them shrug their shoulders wondering why
i tell them *go take a hike- not today*
every day is so vastly different from the other
sometimes i'm thinking
about everything i've missed out on
other times i'm glad i missed those chances
who would i be if i showed up not knowing who i am
well it definitely would've made it harder
for me to appreciate everything i see
sometimes there are clouds in my sky
others time i'm looking in the mirror
thinking about *how lucky i am*
it took me awhile to face the denial
i shake the hands of my past and smile

in memory of us.

i remember when you
told me that you were
always going to be there
for me
and now i'll sit on my porch
watching you make memories without me

the light in the tunnel.

trying to train my brain not to be so distraught
trying to think about all these thoughts
therapy isn't easy but i know giving up is
that's why people give up
that's why when the pain feels like enough
people say *that's enough*
when all you ever wanted was to be okay
you don't want people saying things will be okay
when they are not
sometimes nothing is okay
something nothing goes your way
in a world where everyone wants you to accept it
each time life comes after you in a fit
but i'll give each person i meet the benefit
because i know what it's like to drive in your car
and feel like you just don't
have the answers anymore
it's a hard pill to swallow
when you're thinking about all these things
like what you have to get done tomorrow
but maybe things can actually be okay
maybe if i focus on today
i'll make it another day
and think about all the things if i wasn't here
that everyone would miss
everything that has the ability to give me bliss
you make your marks on someone
everywhere you go
a simple hello or a smile or even your sadness
you have quality and you have substance
let yourself go the distance

what really tied me up
to an anchor and threw me over
wasn't what he did to me
it was what it did to you
what you said
what it did to make
others see me the way you do
it wasn't the fear
i was being groomed
being disposed of
being useless
it was feeling gross in my skin
feeling sorry for myself
feeling bad for being me
feeling bad for what i felt that i did

let me be enough.

i later realized how much
i struggled with my own identity
it was some kind of crisis
trying to figure out through all these vices
when time and time again
the reflections in my hand
weighted on rooms where i was just something
not someone
weighted rooms of needing to be a flower
in all these broken flowerpots
torn and torn between the fine lines
the ones you drew in sand
the ones written all over my hands
who am i and who will i be
reflections of what you'd expect of me
explain to me this destiny
where i am sitting someplace trying to understand
who i am
when all i've been is what you've expected of me
with each dying dream finds the pursuits
of my dreams flourishing
why must i sit someplace wondering about it all
was it even enough
nothing could amount
as sand falls between my fingers
watching things slip away from me
so i can sit back and ask who i am
it's a cycle some cannot break
we do not understand when all we know
is being enough for others
what about being enough for yourself

the ill-timed spring.

i didn't want to talk about it
i had nothing to say
maybe if i stuck it out
without a pout
things could've been okay
i would've figured things out
all while i watched the clock
the secrets kept tightly behind a lock

the silence of my tears.

i remember so many times
people said *everything happens for a reason*
can you explain to me why i deserved to suffer
why i cried tears during my childhood
and people have continued to be so unkind
i'm human and i feel like that's the worst part
of me is *how much i care*
i wonder if god is near
when i was a child and he didn't hear me
i wonder why god left me out
deserted me and everyone else
children don't deserve pain or suffering
those kinds of things lead to conflictions
the kind of pain that can't be undone
isn't it funny how one day you wake up
10 years went by like it was the other day
yet i've still got tears in my eyes
i don't want to hurt you while i hurt myself
i don't want you to know what i'm all about
i'd rather stand out in the rain
while holding your umbrella and
all i've known is finding comfort in the rain
while the kids run around and play
i'll be inside holding my head in my hands
while grief preys on my once blinded eyes
take me with you
so i don't have to live another day without you
i'm just a child who has no clue

to miss the living.

part of me wishes you happiness
the other part of me wishes you sadness
wishes that you'll never get over me
you'll never get over what you lost
when you had me
i want you up contemplating what you said
i want you reminiscing about what you did
but likely you never will
and that's something i get to live with

just because someone's dead
doesn't mean you'll ever get them
out of your head
i've tried many times to just point a finger
tell you- *get out this isn't a pitty party*
others would laugh as i pout
while they sit inside drinking hot chocolate
with their mother
they'd say i resonate with them
like we two we are both the same
when they asked me about mine
just so i can tell them *she's dead*
it makes people uncomfortable
so they stop asking me that question
maybe they'd stop comparing themselves to me
like maybe *i should be so grateful for what i have*
even though time wasn't on my side
like i should reshuffle my card deck
and toss the bad one's out like a rotten egg
like i should just stay quiet after the few
years go by while it's still sitting there
waiting so it can eat me up on the inside
i have unresolved everything
it can't be resolved because i don't have you
telling anyone to *just move on*
is the sickest game i'll never play

eating at my leaves.

it eats at you
day to night
you'll think about it
consistently
until you squash
it like a bug
on a rug

if you prefer
loneliness
to me
i'll leave you alone
i'll leave you be
i'm not chasing your love

can't fit in in the meadow.

they told me to write it down and burn it
but i never did
i let it burn inside me instead
i let my dreams wilt at my fingertips
sadness and abandonment
lingering in between my lips
do i part ways without you
even when i know i'm nothing without you here
you're all the wrong colors
when i'm needing you near
you're all the wrong colors
drawing out my biggest fears
if i just leave you here i'm afraid
my worst fear will come true
after all-*maybe i'm wrong*
about everything that you do
i'd give you the benefit for some time
let the clock wind up overtime
until time and time again
i find myself making excuses for your abuse
you're all the wrong tones
when all i'm needing is a home
you turn the lights off when i need them on
so i don't get lost
you set me on fire and watch me burn
you let my anger turn to rage
then you go and walk away
my mind tells me to stay away
my heart tells me stay
tug of war tug of war i can't understand
how you get the best of me in the end

the turn of events.

a room full of your disappointments
while i feed them down to the bones
hospital beds where you'd cry
let you take your ego with you
let you take your laughter
and remember when each time you cry
before they pull your cord
and let you die
be the shards that you get a chance to walk on
remember that glass i walked on
i'm not too worried about this anger
fueling through my blood
part of me cared but that's the gravestone out back
like the bottom of that 2019 bottle i chose
i hope you prick those fingers
on those photographs
that you hold underneath buried in totes
like the times i loved you and i used to write you
all of those notes
forget the memories
the ones now i spit on
while the crying little girl stands by
she looks shocked *but i'm not*
that's the old me *but still me*
look in the mirrors but they don't reflect
inside this sanity living room
the problem ain't me but what i felt all those times
walk closer and closer to death
let that ego take your fate

when everyone left and the night was silent
i was holding you in my arms
despite everything that i saw that hurt me
i just want to be your warm blanket
your light in the darkness
i'd do anything to make you better
i'd do anything to take your pain
and lock it in a box some place
i'd go out in the night and take your
box of sadness and throw it off a bridge
let me figure out how to help you
so i can help me
i can't fix everyone and i can't even fix me
maybe it's much better to just say
i'll be damaged goods forever
so i stop having some unrealistic expectation
that i can fix what's really on the inside

blaming stages of grief.

before you knew it we were older
so much older
memories kept fading away everyday it seemed
there was no rest that could make me comprehend
how i'd be able to live without you
headstones and erns
i don't want to go visit you
i want you to be here
i don't want to go buy you flowers
i want dinners with you
i don't want to leave gifts at your grave site
i want you to open them infront of me
so i can watch your smile
all i have now are these fleeting memories
of the person you were when you were here with me
when we were children
i never thought you'd become a memory
i thought you'd always be here
i never thought i'd be holding these photographs
i thought you'd still be here taking photos with me
now look at me
longing for a mother i'm stripped away from
stripped away from all the things i cannot have
isn't that the truth
i used to blame god
like how could he have done that to us children
if god exists why would he do such a crime
but blame does nothing for me
i have to swallow this truth

when everything changed.

i always think about child you
and *what happened to make you*
who you are today
i wondered about what dreams you had
how as an adult when i seen you cry
your tears were so painful
pouring out from your face
it was as if you were terrified of me seeing you
now i'm looking at you seeing how easily
you could've been my best friend
how you could've been someone so great to me
and how in this world we never had that chance
because maybe you were held in dark rooms
or maybe someone just pushed you out
when you felt hopeless or worthless
whatever happened to you *i'm sorry*
but i'm mostly sorry for us in the way
that we don't get the chance this time
we won't be anything because of these things
because when i smile i can't let you
keep me without the light
if i abandon myself for you *i'll never respect you*
i hope someday you can figure out
what really happened and
how you became this way

when i just stopped time and held the hands
of the clock just so i could learn how to love you
when i just stopped comparing us
to everyone else
and started living in the moment with you
i waited forever for a love like us
someone that i know i could trust
and when i trusted you and opened up my heart
things haven't been perfect
but i'll be yours from this life to another
when i asked you what happens to us
when we die i wondered
if you wanted me in this life to the next
because that's how much i love
i'll never have any regrets
i've forgiven you quite a few times
just like you've forgiven me
5 years go by and i know you're the one for me

the both of us.

time never let up when you left
it just kept going and going
throwing me left and right
the reasoning for me becoming who i am today
was based on the things that happened to you
before you left
you made me the healer
now i wear your laugh and your smile
i wear my heart on my sleeve
i couldn't distinguish between the both of us
for some time i felt i was living in your skin
i was living this life like it wasn't my own
i just wanted you back
wanted you to come back
but you couldn't so with every piece of myself
i was bringing you back
in every way since your death

the deal for centuries.

i'm the keeper of your secrets
even when we are in deep
bad terms of good terms
but we can't take turns
you'll use them against me
spill all the tea
when you hate me

and then she still worried about
if she was just a body
regardless of the modesty
a mirror image to them
just like anybody else
something to be seen
something to be felt
even when love was dealt

did they see her breathing
did they notice anything

did they know she spoke words
just like everyone else

more than just a body
and then onto someone else

fake trees.

don't confuse words
for reality
many are pretending
to be things
posing amongst one of the trees

the string of loneliness.

maybe loneliness is love
i guess that's what i've considered my grief
the loneliness of sitting on the steps
of my porch waiting for time to pass
while you're no longer here with me
maybe loneliness is our shared experiences
in all of these shared memories
the ones of you and me
when times were much simpler
i was unbothered by the thoughts
of who i would lose
losing a mother
losing a friend
losing a family member
those things felt long distances away
seemingly another world to me
i wish i could keep it that way
now here they are with me
when i'm having coffee in the early mornings
when i'm driving home most days
somedays i don't think too much
but somedays i think of this loneliness
the reality of these parallel universes

burying my boundaries.

then i realized pretty quickly
if you could've chosen
you would've chosen things differently
you couldn't choose
it was a balance between
every single thing you would lose
when it comes to loving you
i'm not choosing to lose

just to carve you out.

insecurities
i wonder what they do
asking you all these questions
just to figure out what you'll do
i can trust others
but i'll wonder just how long
it'll take until they sneak their way in
sneaking into my heart
then like a snake injecting venom
you'll teach me again how that wasn't smart

when i see her turn her head
here she goes
she goes again
coming right back to him
the fall never lasted long
the summers shorter
each time around
i wonder how she felt
when she left him
what cards were dealt
just tell me why
why did you run away
then come right back around

i always loved messy over clean slates
the damaged people have to be my favorite
maybe it's because they understand
my suffering and we can laugh together
versus them trying to fix the brokenness in me
i don't want to be fixed with pills or therapy
because i've tried for years
and it doesn't work for me
you can't fix what's under my skin- *stop trying*
i've numbed myself out with alcohol or pills
trying to find anything to suppress
how it is i really feel
we all hide behind something and what i hide
behind is what i saw
don't ever say you know how i feel
while i'd scratch an itch but
at least it wasn't on my skin
it was in my skin
inside me

i realized
good friends were few and far
people will forget you
people will leave you asking *why*
people will stop asking
what's going on with you
how you're feeling
how you're doing
people won't stay up at night
anymore
calling you
thinking about you
you become a small memory
a small piece of something
that once was
yet you worry
about *what could be*

i remember years ago
and i think about our jokes
someone told me
that you've woke up
and now you don't even
remember
me

buckets of hatrid.

then after awhile
she didn't understand
how did they hate her so much
and want to make her sad
sitting alone
wondering
how they thought she had the
courage to make decisions
the strength to just leave

the weight of my mistakes.

when each day comes to an end know
i was ashamed of my own shadow
scared that whenever or wherever i grew
that i was really scared of turning
into the monster i knew
i'm not a perfect person and more than likely
that won't ever be true
but when i put a mirror up
and face myself
i wonder what voids i was filling
they tell me make sure to fill my cup
meanwhile i was running on empty
wasn't loving myself
wasn't choosing peace over chaos
i'm still looking for answers
still searching for reasons *why*
i had so much to be happy and grateful for
but when the lights turned off
i could see my wrongs and guilt consumed me
i seen how i was so great but so destructive
full of sadness in my heart
i'm trying to take steps forward
holding all this weight in my arms

moving on from things.

forgiveness was always hard
it was like salt to a wound
but forgiving you
means forgiving myself
for the time
i didn't know how to let you go
the times i didn't let you leave

my mistake
wasn't the one spoon feeding your sorrow
my mistake only helped bring it out
make it sting
helped you realize what you lost in the end

the master manipulator.

you're the abandonment wound
the turn of the story
when the one's closest to her
didn't deserve a chance
i swear i wouldn't have know it
at first glance

you got to know my mom
got to know me
i won't forget what you did
to her and to me
you didn't deserve us
you didn't deserve our trust
i'm glad it's mutual now
now that we became dust to dust

she would want me to be strong
because that's what she taught me all along
i know that she will forever be in my heart
and that we will never be apart

unreciprocated.

old friends forgot about me
life kept moving
i was spinning around backwards
trying to get attention from you
wondering how history kept repeating itself
it had to have been some kind of joke
but it wasn't
i find books and letters that i wrote to you
now i sit here wondering why i wasted this time
all the time i had in my hands
on people who disposed of me easily
realizations come to me
i was a good friend lost in the wind
lost in my head
lost in all the jokes that were once told
growing up–all of us little kids
i stopped laughing like i used to
nothing was funny anymore
my mental health problems consumed me for years
just me and all my darkest fears
bad decision after bad decision
i had to learn who was really there
open your eyes
and you'll see who is really there

when i saw you the last time
i can admit everything was not fine
to touch your hand
cold
and i misunderstood
why did you leave-
at this moment
make-believe

i'll go cry in the rain now.

i'm crying now because
you let me go-
without even knowing
how much i loved you

out of the dungon.

i woke up one day and said
i'm going to speak up
i'm done playing
the silent game
think what you want say what you want about me
i'm the loud daughter i do the unspeakable things
by coming infront of your face
giving you a taste of your own reality
no one likes the truth at the end of the day
everyone loves circuses and plays
the candy you get from a parade
today is not the day
but i'll move on after everything i have to say
i won't let you make me stay
i won't let you smother me with sadness
mold me up with such terrible clay
i'm not insane and i'm not a terrible person
i'm not what you say i'm not even bad
i'm just mad at you for trying to make me that way
i'm mad you won't sit there at take it
after i took it for years and you know exactly
what i am talking about right now
just sit down i would say as you keep trying to get up
out of your seat because you can't take it
just sit down
just take a glimpse into what happened
behind these eyes
just sit down so you can welcome yourself
into the streams of all your lies
that you tried so deeply hard to leave behind
inside my eyes

everyday it rained.

how could i
have ever understood love
when i was the one
wiping tears from her face
i act like i'm emotionless
when deep down i'm full of emotions
i say *i'm okay*
when i'd much rather cry
it comes from the time i held you
it comes from being me and being the one
who gets to carry around kleenex
in the sleeves of my pockets
now i carry your photo around in a locket
i'm supposed to heal everyone
when all that's left is to heal me
i'm supposed to meet everyone half way
but i'll meet you all the way
i'll give up every inch and every speck
and every grain of my being
just to give you the solace you crave
i'll hold you when you cry
but forget to hold myself until the day i die
tell me why i am this way

artificial flowers.

why was it that
no matter what i said
you couldn't love me that way
you know-
the way you loved them
i don't even know
if you ever loved me
i don't want you to tell me
i'm just going to go on now
this is the end

i can't keep your dirty secrets.

it's so disturbing what you did
how they told me i was lying
when i was sitting there
wondering where you were
i knew you were broken
but why me
why am i your albi
why does my skin
feel like a crime
i've never felt lower than that
i was so young
knowing that you did that to me
it made me drive home
silently
asking what even happened
why it went that way
unspeakable
unheard of
i'm just a cover-up for you
the keeper of your secrets
while you keep all my regrets

just like the wind.

i wish i could turn off the switches
deep in the chambers of my heart
where i see your face and i feel nothing
if i could i would
i would think
what a psychopath
what a nutjob
but i'm not her and she is not me
i wonder how you've been
i wonder if life has been kind to you
i hope time heals you
i wish good for you
while you wish down on me
i still wonder about things
there's no sense wondering about
i still love you
even when there is no sense in
loving someone who hates me

i felt for awhile
we were all options
something to be kept
or something to be disposed of
my body wasn't my temple
it mean't nothing to me

people care.

you never know how much you mean to someone
i've met people once and wondered
what made them as special as they are
how their souls were lighting up
filled with love and hope
you leave marks on people's hearts
even when you're unknowing
the kids i found crying in the bathrooms at school
the kids i found alone listening to music
wondering what they were going through
people care about you even when you don't know it
people are curious about the deeper parts of you
the one's that you've kept hidden away
the one's tucked away in unhappy homes
oh-all the joys stolen from all of us
thinking no one's thinking about us
late night someone is probably thinking of you
wishing you well
wishing you happiness
meanwhile you're battling your demons
battling all these hardships
trying to glue back these pieces
the one's that are keeping you from falling apart
when your world stops
people wonder about where you are
when your world stops
people wonder about your spark
grow through your thorns
embrace your spark

only a matter of time.

i miss your laugh
how you spoke
i can't remember you much anymore
i find that the more days
the more years passing by
they steal each memory
they steal you away from me
my mind plays tricks on me
making me forget you

let the sun shine.

honey bee
you're a flower
but they wouldn't let you bloom

see
i felt worse for her
even though she was alive
what she is a dealt
is a greater suffering than
someone else
they ask me
how does she still tolerate that
i respond
i'm really not sure
they look confused
i'm not
all i have to say is
she got what she wanted
but inside *i feel bad for her*
not pity
just some kind of sadness
a deep reminder
of the memories
that restructured my heart

don't force it.

i don't know why
i didn't understand it sooner
i didn't get it
why i was all messed up
torn up over people
trying to fit puzzle pieces
in the puzzle where
they didn't even belong
hung up on the fact
they didn't want to fit in that puzzle anyways
i'm done yelling at the puzzle pieces
tossing them around
trying to jam them in someplace
when i'd never understand how
wondering why in the world
they just won't fit
why can't they just fit perfectly
seamlessly
it's just impossible
now i have to start all over with the pieces
the one's i do have while i still have them
all here infront of me in my hands
take all my gratitude and let it fill my cup
with a smile on my face i can accept what i have
and acknowledge what i don't have
and break the silence with the peace of being me
all these puzzle pieces
all fitting perfectly and seamlessly
these are the ones for me

each time i forgave you–
i forgave you
and broke a part of me
it was the way of ruining myself
just to please you
just to get acknowledgment
it was that i never knew
how to even love me
how to even care about me
that day when everything changed
i found out the hard way
i live my life like i live in a play
i live my life like i won't be living many more days
you made me only care about this moment
where i would self-destruct
it's a self-harm construct
i'll hurt me just to get back at you
self-fulfilling prophecy just to make sure you lose
well
each time i lose too
walking around with this abandonment wound
the last thing i really had to do
was cut you off completely
from the knowing and the unknowing parts of me
you weren't coming around
all that's really left is learning how to be found
i can't get this from you so i'll let go of your arms
so you can stop me from doing all of this harm
the blood is on your hands
finally the deepest part of me can understand

twisting the vines.

in another life
my mom was able to continue living hers
my friends never lost their lives
all the people around me didn't suffer
unspeakable traumas
pushing things under and out
holding it all inside
my mother had found a love
one that she deserved
i never had to move on without my loved ones
who had me living a full life
in another life no one died
everyone survived the things
the battles they faced were conquered
a twist of fate changes
the one where no one is complacent
where no decisions are made
to leave the world or to move on to the golden gates
early morning drives
late nights when i'm squirming in my bed
i live a half a life without all of the pieces
that made me whole on the inside
so now all that's left is to hold and honor
the one's that i have
i don't get another chance
none of us do

crushing expectations.

i finally stopped caring
what other people thought of me
if they felt *i was so odd*
i guess i wouldn't mind being it
if they found me to be terrible
i guess that's terribly great
i wasn't sent here to please anybody
be everyone's cup of tea
i'll just keep being me
don't like my hair
don't like what i wear
i really shouldn't care
i'm no fashion model
i'm not paid enough for this anyways
don't like my hair or what i wear
i just won't care
i keep my eyes on me
because i can't be anything or anyone else
except me and only me
don't like my mistakes
point fingers at me
each time like you've never made a mistake
but i'll keep giving myself grace
because i walk in these shoes
i know what all of this feels like
how at my lowest i had to muster up the fight
just to get to this good place
if you were me
you'd be too coward to show your face
couldn't be me though
i can take all my mistakes and give them a taste

tackling the shame.

you can't tackle trauma
shaming yourself to death
that's what i've learned
i've shamed myself to death
i'm not planning to keep the shame forever
but i'd often put myself in front of a target
i'm my own target on my back
and let a shotgun do the rest
that's unfair
come on
really really really
unhelpful too
maybe it's much better to say
i've done bad things but i'm not a bad person
or maybe i've had a few miscalculations
i've went overboard off my paddleboat
something like that sounds a little better
so long as i learn from my mistakes
own them
be accountable of them
see myself as a human being
because that's all i can be is a human being
i have blood in my skin
i'm human and oh–
remember that you're human too

when i see you passing me by
i pretend not to notice you
i wonder if you still have my mother's
things posted up somewhere
someplace in your home
while you hold your judgments
of her daughter
ever so tightly in your arms
do you clench your fists with hatred
despising every piece of me
i know you believe that you know me
even though you'll never know me
do you talk to my mother
as you look at her photographs
all those judgments
just to try and tell a mother
where her daughter has a place
know that the only place
you'll take up any space
is buried in the backyard
of my memories
the one's where i realize
within the space of our distance
within the reality of our differences
all this time who you truly are
i won't forget it but i forgive it
so that i can move on to bigger better things
things you'll never be apart of

i just wanna know
what it's like for you
when you're laying up at night
are you grieving us
grieving all we used to be
the really sad part of it all is
that you forgot about me so easily
just as natural as you blink your eyes
how i spent so much time on you
just for you to betray me and my time
maybe you were comfortable
as comfortable as can be
snuggled into blankets somewhere
knowing you lived with your family
it didn't bother you that others were temporary
when you said you'd love me forever
then you chose boy after boy over us and me
i knew they would hurt me
but i had no idea you would hurt me
now i turn to the page of my story
where i decided to be left alone
sticking to the ones who stick with me
telling myself desperately to leave the rest alone
the older i get the more i've learned
to stop beating myself up over responses
i've had from everything that they did
responses coming from the stream of lies
responses coming from the stream of denial

the ruthless bathroom scene.

when the conflict became
she didn't like me
i wanted to be her friend
then she said what she said
did what she did
that broke me in the end
made fun of my hair
the shoes i would wear
if i stood in a room with her
i would wonder
why my very existence was thunder
what did i ever do to her
to make her hate me so much
it wasn't enough either
because she had to do it again
and again
until one day
i told her my truth
i wonder would she
have thought twice

deep down
it really pains me
it really caused a battle within me
how you caused me to suffer
with those insecurities
i would chase it around
even when you were never around
when you spoke such
terrible words to me
and my voice went unheard
leaving that home with tears in my eyes
telling you truths that you always deny
the excuses for the bruises
that you left in my heart
there are no conversations
only such massive frustration
that you didn't see the tears in my eyes
the only one knowing was my foundation
where you stuffed pain into the pockets
of every single pore
every crevice
every sore

when you get what you want.

let me get a book
so i can decorate the parts of myself
that came from the deeper parts of you
let me print out photographs
when you would pose and pretend
when you acted like you were okay
but under it all the family was the pain
if i live in a home that's burning on fire
i'll probably always be tired
when your eyes matched the energy
and your soul lost it's chemistry
it was within your eyes
here lies the blessings of a picket white fence
here lies the blessings of a ring
when the hurt began at the fingertip
dirty water river edges it was at the root of a stream
i can't unsee the fakeness of it all
the smell of burning food in an oven
that you forgot about like you forgot about
all the times that you couldn't find love
within those with tainted hearts
within those with such bleak remarks
you can't love a liar just like you can't love
when your home burns in the fire
the fire where he laid just so he could consume
victims with every muscle of desire
let me turn to the pages when you prick
my fingers and i have paper cuts
from every single remark
every fiber of my being came from these things
defining moments of my being

i have memories
from when i was a kid
you made me understand
my dreams
my pursuits
everything you did
i was always a giver
because you gave your all to me

you are filthy take a bath.

i remember the invasion
all the conversations felt like persuasion
i was supposed to be something
something i wasn't
someone that doesn't do those things
but when i tried so hard to scrub it off
i realized it wasn't coming off
i can't take it away
i can't be what you wanted
your body is your temple
i was completely daunted
it just stuns me
it taunts me
how you said what you said about me
when i was only a teen

willow trees.

i still have a lot of your things
things you gave me that made me smile
cards you gave to me on birthdays or valentines day
that scrunchie you gave me that i love
the one with all the sequins on it
you always knew how to bring a smile to my face
i miss baking those cookies
sitting around talking about life with you
now i talk about a life that i don't have with you
the laughter i can no longer hear
your voice and the grief i can barely bare
and when you died a part of me did too
because i can't find you in anyone else
i can't look for you in someone else
it's not possible for there to be someone like you
all i have are the things and the moments
that'll never be enough
when you love someone so much
all i can do is hold the memories close
and hope that in another life i'll be seeing you
that we get a chance to make more memories
someday
someplace

ticking time bomb.

i've done terrible things
my guilt and shame say to me as it eats away at me
and makes me cry
i used to think my addictions
loved me more than anyone else ever could
i felt stupid like i should have known better
i should've known all my problems
would come right back to me
it was really difficult for me to unpack my suitcase
and look at all the terrible things
i did to myself
i've always been at the root of my own suffering
i've always know right from wrong
but still taken the wrong paths
i cried and screamed
wondering why
i would even do this to myself
but i heard the whispers and chose different
i felt conflicted but put my self on the stand
i am my own witness
if i want to live i must learn to live different

the sweet taste of revenge.

and if my trauma had a flavor
or a taste
i wonder what you would think
if it was in your mouth
would you take back what you did
would you take back what you said
would you spit it out or
would you hold it in your mouth
would you have regret
would you flinch
would you see yourself as a threat
tell me
what would happen differently
but it's something that you can't do
you can't take any of it back
you can't make any of this okay
you'll live with it for the rest of your days
that makes me happier
knowing that even though i'm hurt
that you live with the hurt you gave me
there's no better revenge
than the silence i give
there's no better revenge
than sitting back and letting
you find out the hard way
when it's only you
sitting alone in the end

i wanted to be beautiful like my mother
i loved her calmness and her fashion taste
she was kind
she was loving
everyone seen her as extraordinary
i'd watch her at her vanity as she applied
her makeup or her lashes
she was a giver
because she knew what it felt like
to be wounded
she was so beautiful
stringing together everyone else's pain
she'd put you together as good as new
she was a giver
she made a giver out of me
my mother was beautiful
she is beautiful
she lives on in me
she lives on in my brothers
she lives on in my family
some people are the glue
the invisible strings
that tie us all together forever

when it was time to let go.

i forgave you exactly a dozen times
i wasn't really keeping count in my head
it was in my heart
where i wondered
where and when it would all end
when you told me all those times
how awful i was
when you threw away my things
you were addicted to conflicting me
that can't be love
every time you moved
you moved on without me
you left me and left my things behind
you've always been so unkind
i used to chose a lot of men who were like you
i remember everything that was said
it was only when i finally let you go
that i found all the love that i really needed
i found that you were never there all along
i was lonely even when i had so many
circling all around
the loneliness stung and the lack of love
the lack of everything that you never gave
i don't regret it and i won't regret it
i won't put on fake smiles or believe you
i won't do things just to make people feel better
when i'm around you i will never get better
i can't grow with you so i'll outgrow you
the only thing left is for me to forgive

burned time and time again.

my once beautiful leaves
my once growing roots beneath
you've torn my branches
you've ripped away my leaves
you've burned me
you've deprived me of water
and kept me from the light
now i'm rotted
broken
and struggling to breath
but that's what you wanted from me
you love depriving me of everything
you love making me second guess
every single thing
you appreciate

gone too soon.

there your beautiful body
is laid to rest
i try to keep calm
others are talking to me about memories
others are acting as if nothing happened
i'm in my head thinking to myself
how *i will bury my mother*
why can't she just wake up
open your eyes
please
don't you understand it's too soon for me
don't you know i can't let you go
i can't do this alone
i want to scream
i want to run away from this nightmare
why can't it just be some stupid dream
so i can wake up
when i open my eyes
you're there again
smiling at me

when sadness turns into anger.

i know you're thinking
this won't fall back on you
this won't damage me or do much of anything
but it will
all those mistakes you made will eat you away
i wondered for some time how
someone could torment others for so long
and never feel a thing
you were cold
ice cold
untouchable it seemed
i know the darkest parts are eating you up
somewhere inside there
coming out in your anger
your rage you keep locked up inside

the real time.

i can't move on from who i used to be
the one that i was when i was with you
now you're gone
now what's left is me
who am i and who am i supposed to be
life doesn't hold the same sun without you now
life doesn't hold any of my favorite things
because you were once everything
each time i accomplish something
i think of the time you cheered me on
now all i think about is the people telling me
just move on
i can't move on and i don't want to
i'll dig a hole and bury myself with you if i have to
but i love you so much that i'll continue living
i'll continue living on
i'll think of the comfort i only found in your arms
your laughter and i'll just pretend for a moment
that you're still here
i love you and i know that you really loved me
part of grief is knowing how often i'll feel
like other people don't love me the way you once did
i'm supposed to be happy meanwhile i'm dreaming
i'm dreaming of your warmth and your touch
when i was a child and you tucking me in
i'm supposed to be happy *look at everything i did*
mom do you see it from where you're standing
or is the dividing line between life and death
too high or too far and i'm lonely again
grief is lonely sometimes and other times
it's a reminder that there are no two of you
there are no two of me

the home inside my heart.

you told me if you could go anywhere
you would go to egypt
i was a kid wondering *why egypt*
but you're an artist
the artist of your child's lives
now i see you in my dreams
you finally get to live out your dreams
your spirit isn't trapped inside your body
it's all around us
you're in egypt in the pyramids
loved one's aren't gone *they are apart of us*
they are the life around us
mom isn't gone she's just gone on vacation
she will be home soon
the home inside our hearts
true love never dies
she will be home soon to give me a kiss
she will be home soon to give me a hug
for now- *i'll see you soon*
i'll be seeing you in the sunshine
i'll be thinking of you all my life
good times and bad times
you're the sunshine on my face
you're the home cooked meals
you're in the crowd someplace
when they call my name
i know you're proud somewhere out there
you're clapping and you're crying
all you ever wanted was to be a mother
no one can replace
you're a mother like no other

i'm not keeping this secret.

for a moment i thought that love was
what you were doing to me
each time you peered your eyes to a screen
each time your eyes didn't showcase
what you were doing to me
some people have secrets
others have really large ones
those secrets abuse other people
use other people
dispose of families and relationships
but when you confront them
they disown them
the secrets that were worth so much
become discarded carelessly
leading them to never take ownership
what would your sons think
your daughters think
understand very carefully
that what behaviors and secrets you keep
will not only harm a lover
but greater harm to the children instead
you'll teach them
what you do
they will become a reflection instead
reflecting it and accepting it
it will become a common practice
in their hearts and their heads

i don't do well with loss.

before you know it
here i am putting on black
attending another funeral
when i'd much rather have you here
tears roll down my eyes
all the people now in their seats
wondering why
when you realize everything you love
will eventually be everything you lost
everyone shares the same fate
everyone will eventually die
i can't do open casket
i don't want to see the shell of who you were
i'd rather remember you
when you were lively
when you had a smile
when you had laughter as contagious as ever
rather than wilt at the thought
of your body withering away

i'll never judge you.

the bond between a mother and a daughter
is unconditional
through the trials of life
the brokenness of mistakes
cannot fault the love or take away
i'd never see you differently
because you loved your children
i'd never judge you
because i know about what you did
i'd only intend to understand you
life isn't filled with perfection
it's filled sometimes with so much pain
many of us may suppress the pain
leading that trauma to come back ten fold
until you learn how to handle your trauma
learning from the mistakes
face it all in front of you
you're going to keep reliving those mistakes
you can't be a perfect person
you will make mistakes
you may spend most of your younger years
trying to understand your suffering
you might be feeling the weight of it all
heavy on your shoulders
but please know that life is full of trial and error and
you deserve to be here

when the pain of loss
comes creeping in
but the others intent came clearly
no numbness like the fog in the night
clarity and greed
mustering the courage to speak out
against those who couldn't await
the entitlement was of great fright
they could print it out as an image
looking down at it in their palms
like some kind of sickness was the greed
waiting for the clock to tick
waiting for some sense of entitlement to call
the grief came as covered up
like some kind of coping skill that was enough
the stains on one's heart always turn
at the right moments
questions and trying to make sense of it all
when did the hearts turn so cold
waiting by the clocks
watching their arms like the happiness
and it all goes tick tock
filling the voids and stuffing them all
i'm embarrassed of it all

the hiss in the garden.

if you put me in the room
with all the things i've always wanted to say
i'd tell you the truth
good people are few and far
some of the people you grew up with
end up being snakes in the garden
some of the people you grew up with
you wish you could go back
and make sure they never got tangled up
in branches where they shouldn't be
it might take you years to realize
the true reflection of yourself or the people
who are all around you
even then- you wonder if it's all a dream
you wonder how people are really so unkind
and so entitled underneath the surface
you wonder if the words they speak
even hold much meaning anymore
that's why i now end up staring at the floor
i hate snakes and i hate liars
and i knew you'd hate them too
all people end up revealing their true selves
and when they do remember what you see
tread carefully and trust what they show you
bad times will show you one's
true character
good times will show you the ease of such
comfort from a snake's grip around your waist

i found in all the spaces
that i would become
accepted by following
the guide of my guardian angel
she would hold me as troubled as i am
snuggled deeply into her arms
then from that time i found myself
and all the spaces where i needed to belong
where i needed to be complete
filled with love and joy
there i found the reflections of the years
that quickly passed me by
the years i cried
wondering who i was inside
or what i was made of
flying beside me is my dove
my guardian angel with all her love
all the signs and my comfort from above
thank you for saving my heart
when i felt like i was falling apart

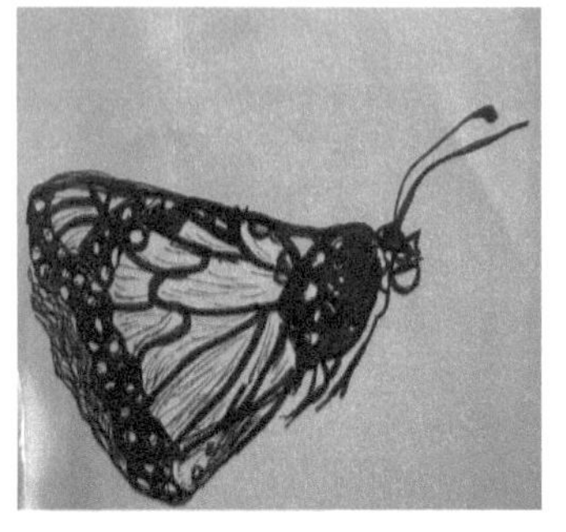

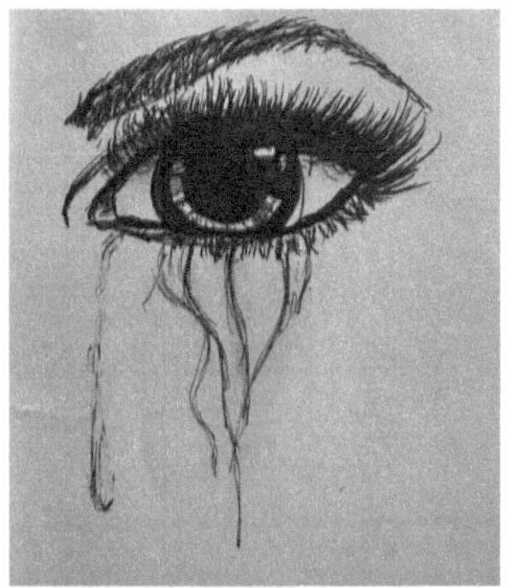

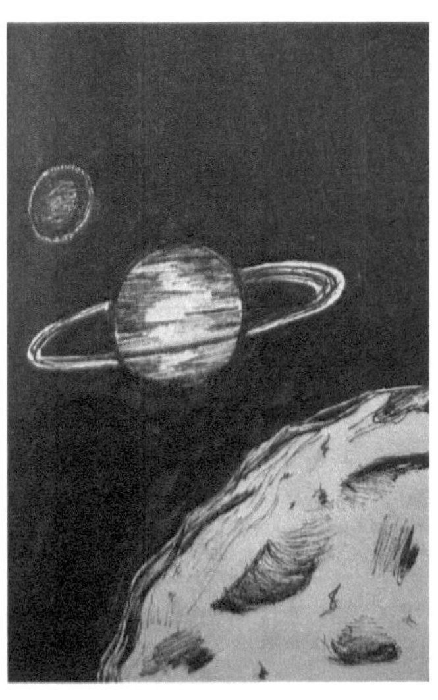

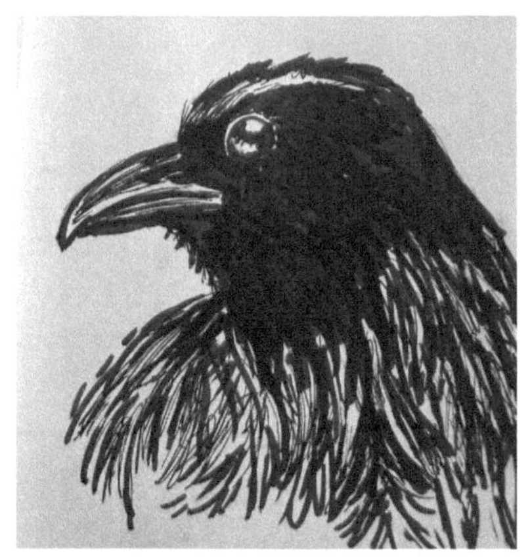

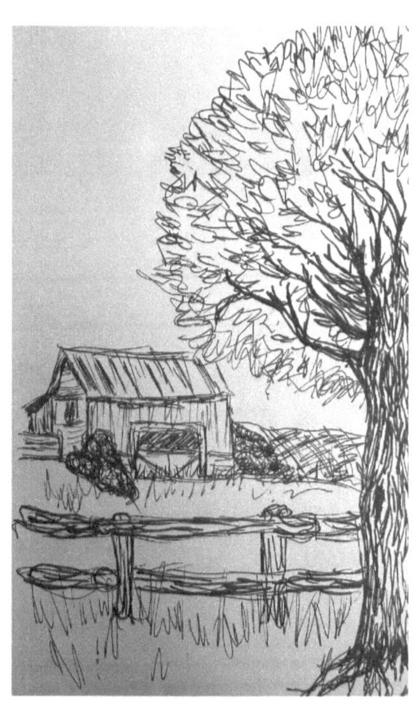

artwork by Kimberly

ABOUT THE AUTHOR

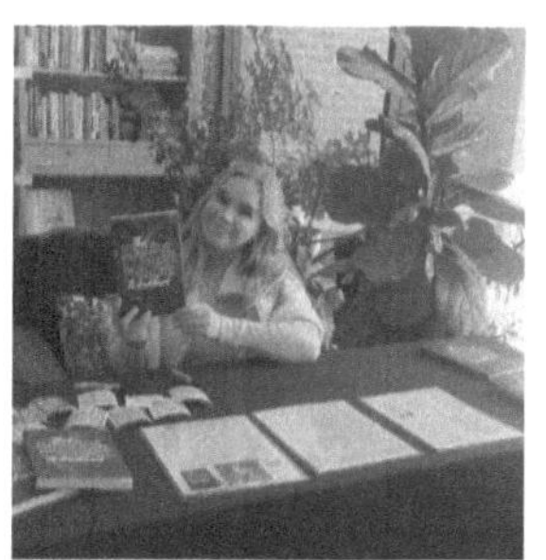

ARIANA ALEXIS TORRENCE

I wrote these poems as a way of storing the recollections of my childhood & adulthood memories, love, and life experiences. I've also gained insight into the ways grief influenced my life in both good and bad ways which led me down many paths to being my own healing to my own worst enemy.

I hope these poems give you the courage to speak your mind and appreciate yourself. I hope when you read these poems to yourselves or your children during trial times you see the courage within yourself and others.

My greatest achievements in life include being a mother, a military veteran, an author, and a clinician in the mental health field. Healing and recovery are possible, never lose hope!

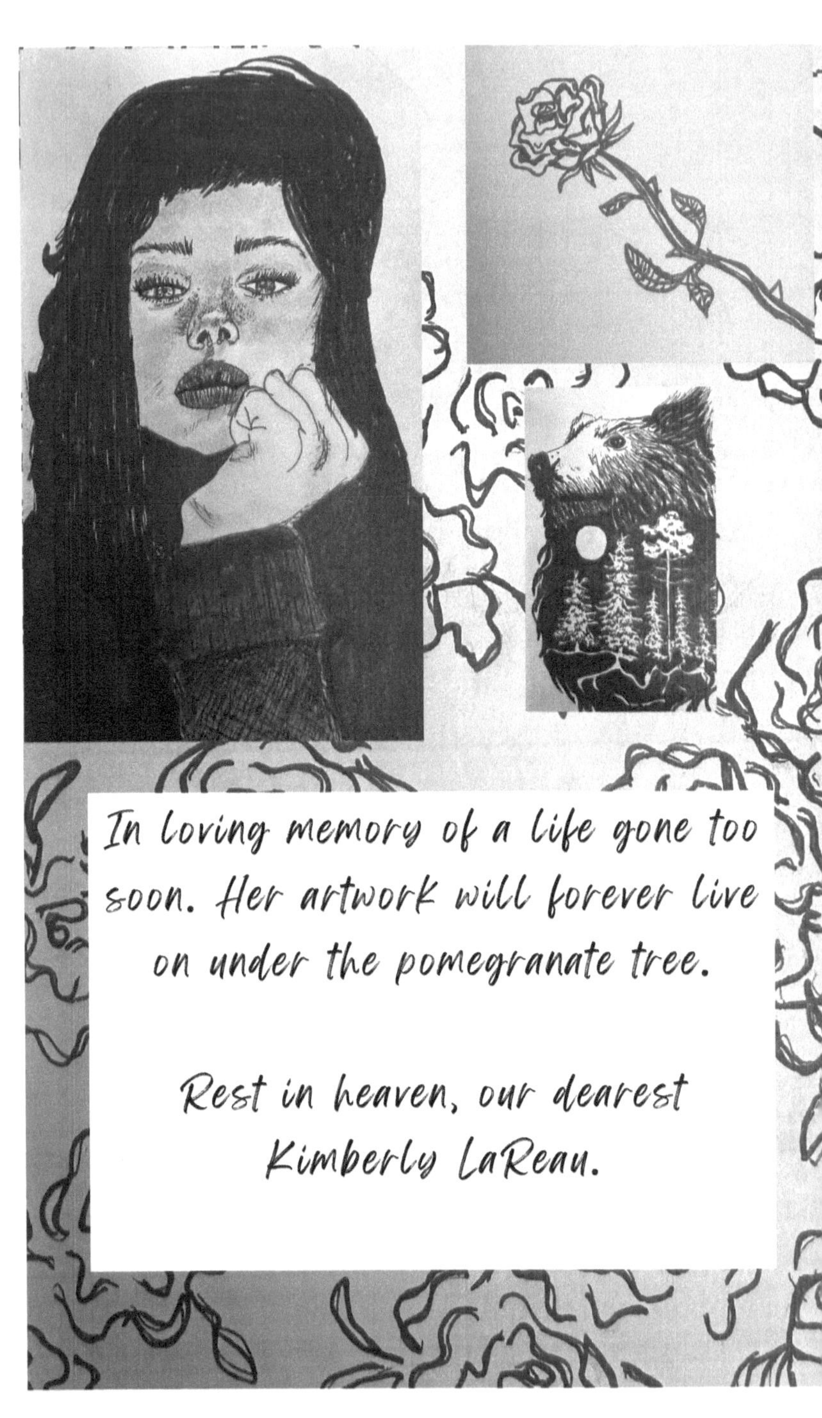

In loving memory of a life gone too soon. Her artwork will forever live on under the pomegranate tree.

Rest in heaven, our dearest Kimberly LaReau.

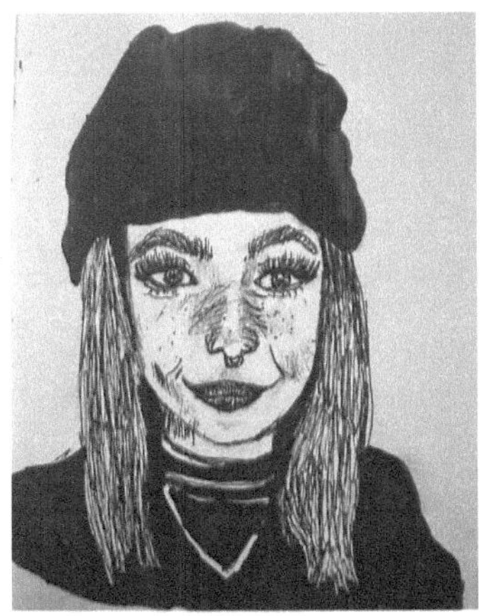

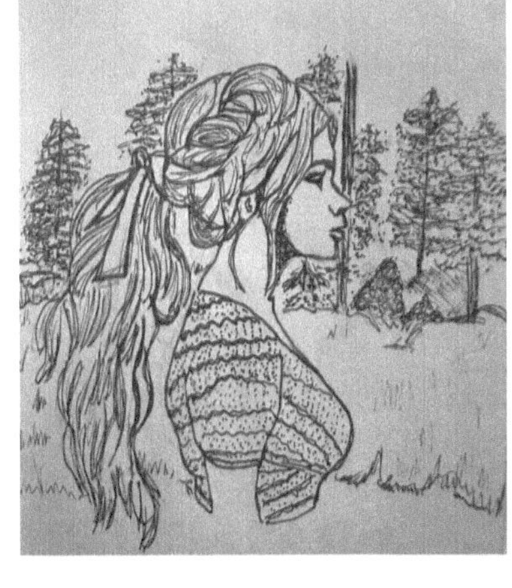

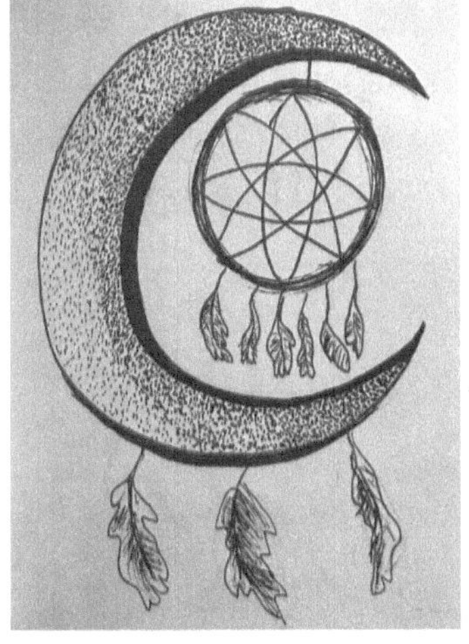

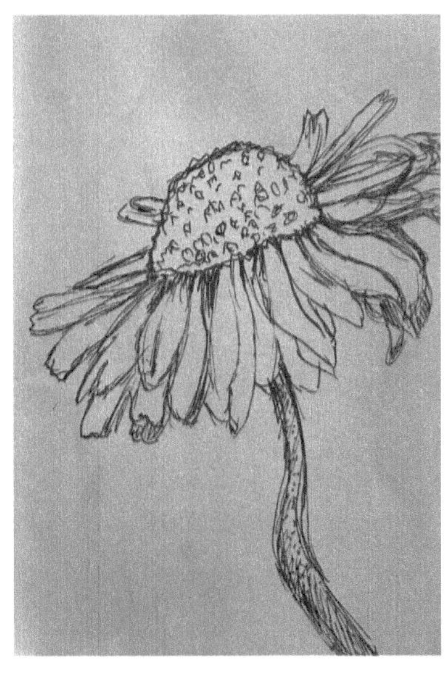

artwork by Kimberly

MORE BY THE AUTHOR:
ARIANA TORRENCE

THE HEALING THROUGH TRAUMA WORKBOOK

AVAILABLE ON AMAZON

you will go on

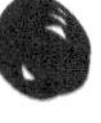